It dedicated in May of 1888 and
finally accepted by the State
of that year. At that time the
value of the panhandle lands put
up by the State as compensation
for the job was less than $2000 000.
The building actually ended up
costing about $3.75 million of which
the State contributed $500 000 in addition
to the land. At the time of the
Capitol Centennial in 1988, the
lands set aside by the Constitution
of 1876 for construction of the
Capitol were valued at nearly $7 billion.

Babcock had actually visited the lands

Texas Past

Texas Capitol at dawn

Texas

ENDURING LEGACY

Past

By Andrew Sansom

Photographs by Wyman Meinzer

Foreword by Lt. Governor Bob Bullock

Edited by Jan Reid

Historical Consultant, Sue Winton Moss

TEXAS PARKS *and* WILDLIFE PRESS

Library of Congress Cataloging-in-Publication Data

Sansom, Andrew.
Texas Past: enduring legacy / by Andrew Sansom;
photographs by Wyman Meinzer; foreword by
Bob Bullock; edited by Jan Reid; historical consultant,
Sue Winton Moss.
p.   cm.
Includes bibliographical references.
ISBN 1-885696-19-1
1. Historic sites—Texas. 2. Texas—History, Local.
1. Meinzer, Wyman. II. Reid, Jan. III. Moss, Sue
Winton. IV. Title.
F387.S26   1997
976.4—dc21   97-36856
                        CIP

ISBN1-885696-19-1

*Costs for this publication were underwritten by
the Parks and Wildlife Foundation of Texas.*

Designed by Barbara M. Whitehead

This book is dedicated
to the
Children of Texas

Holy Cross Cemetery, Yorktown

Contents

Acknowledgments   ix

Foreword   xiii

Prologue   1

CHAPTER ONE   Ancient Texans   5

CHAPTER TWO   Exploration and Colonization   19

CHAPTER THREE   Backwoodsmen, Empresarios, and
Revolutionaries   35

CHAPTER FOUR   Indian Wars   49

CHAPTER FIVE   Ranching Heritage   63

CHAPTER SIX   Melting Pot   75

CHAPTER SEVEN   The Building Years   91

CHAPTER EIGHT   Boom and Bust   105

CHAPTER NINE   Government and Public Buildings   121

CHAPTER TEN   The New Texas   135

Epilogue   143

Bibliography   145

Site Information   149

Acknowledgments

I should write a book about my colleague, Wyman Meinzer. He is one of the most talented photographers anywhere in the world, and his work is only surpassed in its beauty by his own way of life. He is a remarkable human being and a national treasure.

Wyman and I could not have accomplished this second collaboration without the Summerlee Foundation, a unique charitable institution dedicated to history, and the additional funding provided by Anheuser-Busch, which continues to have a significant impact on conservation in Texas. Their support, combined with that of the Parks and Wildlife Foundation of Texas, made this book possible. The Foundation's president, Paula Peters, an historian herself, helped conceive the project, which was produced and directed by Sue Winton Moss, one of Texas' most knowledgeable historians. Neither Wyman or I will ever be able to thank Sue enough. Another stroke of luck for me was that Jan Reid agreed once again to be my editor. He is a pleasure to work with and, more importantly, helps me say what I want to say while making me look like I know what I am talking about. The book's final handsome appearance is due to the efforts of Barbara Whitehead, the accomplished designer with whom we worked before, and Jolley Printing in Houston who did the press work.

At the Texas Parks and Wildlife Department, Michelle Klaus prepared the manuscript, and Anne Helbing coordinated everything together with wonderful Georg Zappler, creator of Texas Parks and Wildlife Press. They, along with the Texas Parks and Wildlife Commission and the Department staff, are the most

Acknowledgments

committed and professional conservationists in America. In fact, under the guidance of leaders like Dr. Wilson Dolman and Dr. Cynthia Brandimarte, the professionals at Parks and Wildlife who protect, manage, and interpret Texas' great historic treasures are the most talented, dedicated, but under-appreciated group of people in Texas. I thank them.

No one understands their dedication and contribution better than our former Commissioner Terry Hershey. She and her husband, Jake, let me retreat to their nineteenth-century German farmhouse at Stonewall for most of the writing.

Meanwhile, at public and privately owned historical places across the state, the following people each made invaluable contributions to this project for which we will always be grateful. It should be said that there are many more historic places in Texas that must be preserved but could not be illustrated on these few pages. Those places and the people who value and care for them are deeply appreciated.

Artie Ahier - *Cibolo Creek Ranch*
Harry Bradley - *Texas State Cemetery*
Pancho Brotherton - *Seminole Canyon State Park*
Ken Brown - *Levi Jordan Plantation*
Jim Bruseth - *Texas Historical Commission*
Halden Conner - *T & P Terminal*
John Crain - *Summerlee Foundation*
Anne Debois - *Governor's Mansion*
Ron Dipprey - *DOW Chemical*
Mr. and Mrs. Otis Gafford - *Gafford Ranch*
Lester Galbraith - *Fort Griffin State Historical Park*
Roy Garrett - *Corpus Christi Museum of Science and History*
Michael Garza - *Fort McKavett*
Mike and Shawna Gibson - *Four Sixes Ranch*
Dr. Tom Hester - *Texas Archaeological Research Laboratory*
Jeff Hutchinson - *Varner Hogg State Historical Park*
David Jackson - *Summerlee Foundation*
Tio Kleberg - *King Ranch*
Moody Mansion and Museum Staff
Michael Moore - *Fort Bend Museum Association*
Jay O'Brien - *JA Ranch*
Mark Peapenburg - *National Park Service*

John Poindexter - *Cibolo Creek Ranch*
Galon Polati - *Dallas Historical Society*
Ken Pollard - *Texas Parks and Wildlife*
Garland Richards - *Fort Chadbourne*
Phillip Riggs - *Caddoan Mounds State Historical Park*
Wallace W. Saage - *Heritage Society of Houston*
Mario Sanchez - *Texas Historical Commission*
Dr. R. G. Sanchez - *San Ygnacio*
Harry Sargent - *Lake Jackson Plantation*
June Secrist - *Landmark Inn State Historical Park*
Carol Stabler - *Wilson Historical District*
Hilton Thompson - *Burton Cotton Gin*
Scott Thompson - *DOW Chemical*
Dr. and Mrs. John Toelkes - *King Ranch*
Ron Tyler - *Summerlee Foundation*
Karen Venetian - *Corpus Christi Museum of Science and History*
Mr. and Mrs. Willis Williams - *Shafter*
Patsy Wood - *T & P Terminal*
Valerija C. Woolvin - *Sisterdale*

Both Wyman and I have understanding spouses, Sarah and Nona. They put up with a lot and our families have grown close in the process. We've been fortunate to work together, to come to know each other better, and to experience together the rich legacy of the Lone Star State.

God Bless Texas.

Foreword

Anyone traveling across Texas today will recognize this place as a living monument to the uncommon courage of the men and women devoted to the land they made their home.

From the prehistoric settlers who left their mark in West Texas, to the modern pioneers who built NASA's communications core at the Lyndon B. Johnson Space Center in Houston, Texans have always taken great pride in stretching the limits of their time and energy to make the most of the vast resources and human potential that have become endemic to the state. After all, some of the most treasured prehistoric cave paintings in the world adorn cliffs over the Rio Grande in Big Bend National Park, and "Houston" was the first word spoken by man on the moon.

In *Texas Past*, Andy Sansom and Wyman Meinzer have taken a rare opportunity to throw open the sash for a glimpse of Texas history through the eyes of the historic sites that stand testament to the transformation of a state and the men and women who built it. These founders were, as the legendary Texas writer J. Frank Dobie liked to say, "carved out of the old rock." They left us their homes and their graves—their footpaths and their forts. But most of all, they left us a vibrant heritage and the backbone to face the future in a state as full of promise as it is rich with the past.

Bob Bullock,
Lt. Governor, State of Texas

Stacked stone fence at Sisterdale, near Fredericksburg

Prologue

For Texans, our greatest asset is our common experience and the unique identity that has been created by our history.

The history of Texas is rooted in the land, and everything that has happened here in one way or other relates to the terrain. The story of Texas is mythic and matches the enormous scale of the landscape itself. Yet it is all the richer for the contributions made by ordinary people of incredibly diverse origin.

Our history is remembered in familiar oft-told tales and other episodes which we have sometimes ignored or been reluctant to face. The story of Texas is very old and it is very new. We have traces of habitation that are as old as any on the continent, dating to the people of the Clovis culture more than 11,000 years ago. Our recorded history began only a few years after Columbus' arrival when, in 1528, storm-battered Europeans first stepped on the Gulf shore. And yet the tumultuous events which define us as a people have all occurred in the span of a little over 150 years.

Historic places are tangible, we can walk up and touch our heritage. Some in Texas are shrines, others are classrooms. Many contain the archives and furnish expositions of proud Texas communities. A lot of them have been lost.

Those which have survived offer our best opportunity to explore and celebrate our unique history and culture.

Thankfully, over the years, many people have stood up for the revered places. Were it not for the efforts of private citizens and descendants' groups, even such hallowed ground as at Alamo Plaza and San Jacinto would have been lost. Today, because of that work, there is a resurgence of interest in Texas' historic places, for they are key components of the state's surging tourism industry.

Apart from economics, these sites supply a living chronology of how Texas has evolved. They are places where fortunes have been made and lost and blood has been spilled. They are locations of spectacular achievements and abysmal failures, of simple truths and subtle meanings, and they are places where our humanity has been most eloquently expressed.

Perhaps because they are so deeply valued, occasionally they have been the focus of conflict that is unworthy of them. What we must achieve is a consensus on which are most important and how we can best protect them.

For a Texas without them is unimaginable.

Texas Past

Shamans in Panther Cave, Seminole Canyon State Historical Park, Val Verde County

CHAPTER ONE

Ancient Texans

We are all immigrants. From the very beginning, all Texans have come from other places. Eons before a sprawling stretch of plains, desert mountains, savannah, and adjoining humid forest came to be known as Texas, ancients moved toward this land on fields of ice. Science cannot say whether these Pleistocene hunters crossed the Bering Strait on floes or on an archaic land bridge. Or exactly when and why they pushed so relentlessly south. Perhaps they were trying to find the end of the glaciers. Whatever moved them, they left traces of their existence throughout North America, but the earliest and most abundant proof that they were here is found on the great steppes of the High Plains and the limestone plateaus of Texas.

These first Texans were hunters of enormous mammoth, bison, bear, and other prehistoric creatures. Today, around the

5

primeval water hole of Lubbock Lake, bones of both humans and beasts present a rich paleo-tableau of their common experience. But in time the glaciers receded, and the last Ice Age ended. With the climatic warmth came harsh necessities of adaptation. The huge animals vanished, and so did the bands of hunters their herds had fed.

The second wave of immigrants also came from Asia. Over thousands of years, they distributed themselves throughout the new land during the period when the flora and fauna we recognize today first began to emerge. Prehistoric Texans were intimately connected with this wildly varied land. And whether they roamed the Trans-Pecos from water hole to water hole, mined and traded flint on the Panhandle's vast short-grass prairies, or built elaborate ceremonial mounds in the shaded Piney Woods, ancient Texans left fascinating imprints of their cultures on the land that sustained them.

By then the western reaches of Texas had already become arid. Life there was terribly hard. In spite of the exhausting demands on their lives—or perhaps because of them—the ancestors of peoples who much later came to be known as Indians composed an illustrated anthology of their knowledge and traditions on cave walls of the unsparing terrain. Though few other artifacts of the Archaic pictograph culture survived, the cave paintings make it clear that this culture was more complex than has been believed. The artists left us their visions of their world and of themselves in the cave paintings; today our challenge and responsibility is to preserve those drawings.

Though beautiful examples of the cave paintings or rock art of early West Texans can be found in the Hueco Tanks formation east of present-day El Paso and in the Big Bend Region, the most spectacular and compelling manifestation of the ancient pictorial expressionism is in the rugged canyonlands where the Pecos and Devils rivers empty into the Rio Grande. Here, shaded from the blistering sun by overhanging rock ledges, literally hundreds of fantastic illustrations evoke an almost mystical insight into the lives, fears, and aspirations of a primitive society struggling both to survive and to express its humanity.

Many eras of cave painting in Panther Cave, Seminole Canyon State Historical Park, Val Verde County

Namesake panther at Panther Cave, Seminole Canyon State Historical Park, Val Verde County

Shamans in Panther Cave, Seminole Canyon State Historical Park, Val Verde County

Three to four thousand years ago, these aboriginal people found sustenance in plants and seeds along with whatever fish and game they could kill. They roamed the bristling terrain during the few rainy months but stayed close to the perennial springs when it was dry. The location of the great sheltering caves was conveyed generation to generation.

When they gathered together for trading, feasting, sport and marriage, the culminating ritual was the ceremonial composition of metaphysical pictographs. Animated by the energy of the festival—and perhaps the hallucinogenic effects of mescal and peyote—celebrants adorned the shelter walls with huge, multicolored murals featuring dominant themes of animal transformation and the ascent of the soul into the firmament.

Hauntingly, the roots of this tradition may be found in similar manifestations in remote Siberia and in the origin of both the name and the practice of shamanism—a belief system in which all living things and earthly objects share a universal spirit. Seminole Canyon contains some of the most powerful representations of shamanistic pictographs. The profusion of painting in the same location over many generations suggests that the act of ritual painting itself was more important to the celebrants than any desire for the marvels to endure. In the famous Fate Bell Shelter, now permanently protected as part of Seminole Canyon State Historical Park, paintings in red, black, orange, yellow, and white are arrayed almost 150 yards along the rear wall of the cave but have almost become completely obscured by continuous over-painting. Elsewhere in the park, and throughout the area of the three rivers, are other masterpieces. The language, customs, and even the name of this culture are lost in time. But what remains is an almost unbelievable legacy of self-expression.

The artistry of ancient people had a practical and commercial manifestation on the High Plains. Along the Canadian River Bluffs is a large deposit of very hard, richly colored flint. For about 12,000 years, indigenous tribes have used this exceptional Alibates flint for weapons and tools. As early as the Archaic period, people maintained well-organized flint-chipping workshops on the hills above the river. By the tenth century

Burial mound, Caddoan Mounds State Historical Park, Cherokee County

10

Petroglyphs at Alibates Flint Quarries, Moore and Potter counties

A.D., the Canadian Valley supported a village culture. These people grew vegetables, cotton, and tobacco. And they mined and traded the Alibates flint.

The miners crafted arrow and spear points and inventive tools—four-bladed knives, two-edged scrapers, and notched hammerstones. They also chipped out chunks, or "blanks" of flint, which they bartered to other cultures throughout the continent. Exchanged for this high-quality raw material were red pipestone from present-day Minnesota, seashells from the Gulf of Mexico and the Pacific, turquoise from New Mexico, and obsidian from Arizona and the Yellowstone vicinity.

Possession of the flint supply was consequently prized. The village culture disappeared about 1450 A.D., and the Alibates quarry was kept open by historic Apaches who moved into the region. After the Apaches were forced out, Comanches, Kiowas, and Kiowa-Apaches utilized the flint. These tribes were nomads, and they trailed the great herds of bison. When the quarry and trade routes languished, the tribes soon found other hard material for their weapons and tools—the metal of European traders and settlers.

First excavated in the 1930s, the quarry's ruins and surrounding vicinity yielded about 16,000 artifacts. Threatened by everything from cattle herding to construction of a new dam, the Alibates site became the cause of an Amarillo banker, insurance man, and archeologist named Floyd Studer. Thanks to the effort and persistence of Panhandle business leaders, the Alibates Flint Quarries were afforded federal protection and became the first national monument in Texas, in 1965. For nearly a thousand years, it had been the center of North America's first arms industry.

While the caves were being painted and the quarries mined, an elaborate aboriginal civilization spread, adapted, and evolved in the woodlands of the vast Mississippi River watershed. Using *atlatls*, or dart-throwers, to kill their game, the Texas Caddos, who were the westernmost extension of this great culture, left projectile points and shards of pottery along the Neches

Fate Bell shelter, Seminole Canyon State Historical Park, Val Verde County

River that go back more than three millenia. Starting in the late eighth century A.D., the Caddoan culture dominated the forests of East Texas for a thousand years. The highly institutionalized society of the ancient Caddos was specialized and hierarchical; different labor forces performed the farming, trading, pottery-making, bureaucratic, and religious functions.

The Caddos made stone axes, longbows fashioned from the iron-hard wood of bois d'arc, finely woven baskets, ornaments of shell and stone, and some of the most superior ceramics found in indigenous North America. But the most distinguishing characteristic of these people was found in their construction of ceremonial earthen pyramids with lengthy stairways leading to sacred temples at the top. Sometimes called Mound Builders, the Caddoan people established trade routes throughout the continent. The sophistication and complexity of their culture were not really known until the mid-twentieth century, when archeologists began to excavate the mounds that early settlers knew as curious landmarks.

The historic Caddos who met Spanish explorers were probably descendants of the early civilization. By then, the Caddos had settled into social patterns so thoroughly congealed that no possibility remained of adapting to hostile challenge. Perhaps the Caddos were too sociable for their own good. Some called each other Tay-sha, or Tejas, a word meaning "friends," and they applied the same terms to the Spanish explorers. But the Caddos' new friends brought diseases against which the indigenous peoples had no immunity, and within a few decades, the splendid civilization and most of its population were decimated. Today, all that remains are a few tribal descendants in Oklahoma, a smattering of artifacts that reflect the masterful traditions of Caddoan art, and the quiet, noble earthworks. In Texas, Caddoan Mounds State Historical Park conducts an active program with school groups, and archeological work continues. But the mystery remains. What happened to the Mound Builders? Where did they go and why?

Against the desert sky at Seminole Canyon, a twenty-two-foot bronze shaman looms out over the revered Fate Bell

Shaman sculpture at Seminole Canyon State Historical Park, Val Verde County

Shamans in Fate Bell shelter, Seminole Canyon State Historical Park, Val Verde County

Artifacts from Caddoan Mounds State Historical Park, Cherokee County, courtesy of Texas Archeological Research Laboratory

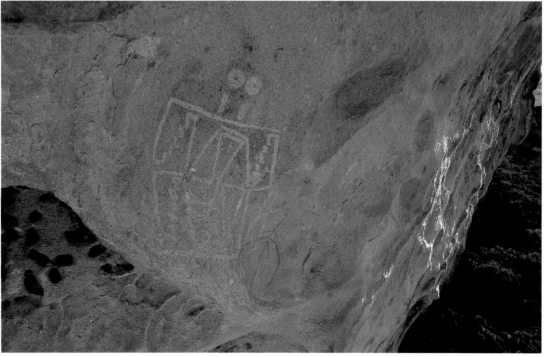

Pictographs at Hueco Tanks State Historical Park, El Paso County

Shelter. Created by modern sculptor Bill Worrell, the work imbues the atmosphere at the state historical park established to protect and interpret the rock art with a consciousness that transcends objective analysis of the great works themselves. The statue was commissioned by a young man from New York in memory of his father, and its execution confirms a transcendent bond between artists of today and the ancient ones.

It is a reminder that we have no higher obligation than protecting the heritage of those who have come before; that we all originally came from somewhere else; that preserved sites like Seminole Canyon and paintings like those of Fate Bell are priceless signatures of humanity; and that saving them for our own children ensures that we will retain at least some of the insights and inspirations of those who went before us so long ago.

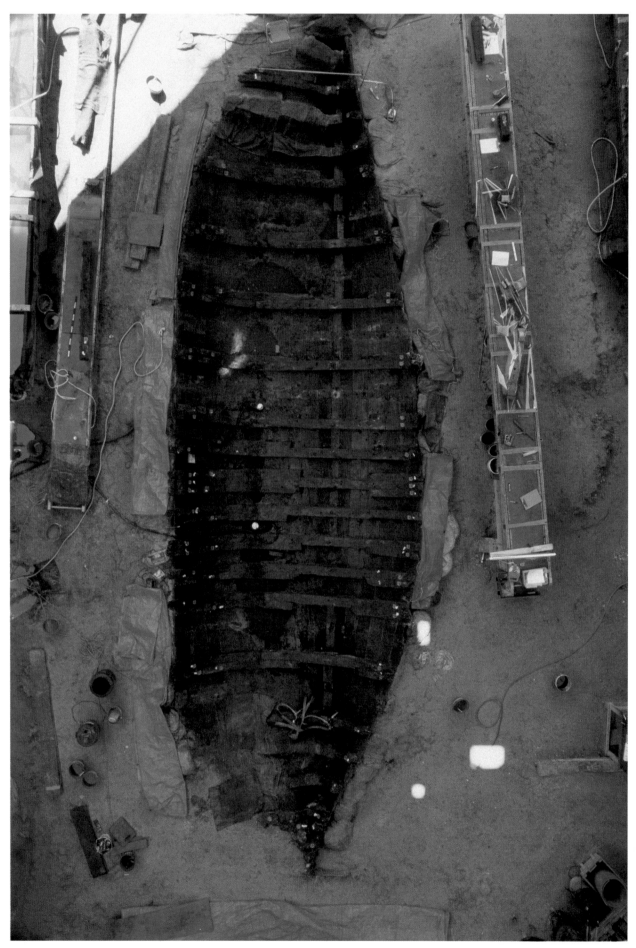

Exposed hull members, La Salle's ship, *La Belle*

CHAPTER TWO

Exploration
and
Colonization

The arrival of the Europeans in Texas was less graceful than that of the ancient nomads. Shipwrecks were the most pivotal feature.

In 1528 a storm in the Gulf of Mexico tossed ashore several rafts of Spaniards including Alvar Núñez Cabeza de Vaca. Most of his shipmates did not survive the terrifying wilderness that came to be known as Texas. But Cabeza de Vaca and three others embarked on an unparalleled odyssey. Staying alive by wit and wile, Cabeza de Vaca was both enslaved by tribes of aborigines and revered as a faith healer and medicine man. He kept moving as a trader, and for six years wandered the plains and bristling desert in search of the countrymen he knew were somewhere in Mexico, then called New Spain. He saw the beautiful Devils River and crossed the Rio Grande at present-day Presidio. He probably encountered the mountainous divide now called El Paso in 1535 or 1536. Cabeza de Vaca survived this incredible experience, and the power of the place and the people he had seen left such an imprint on his being that he wrote *La Relación*. His finely crafted book provided Europeans with their first vivid glimpse of the Americas, and it stands today as one of the great adventure stories in world literature. And it was the first book about Texas.

In the courts and capitals of Europe, the logical extension of support for New World exploration was to claim the land and colonize and exploit it. Based on the tales of Cabeza de Vaca and the later reports of a priest, Fray Marcos de Niza, Francisco Vásquez de Coronado was sent north by the viceroy of New Spain to lay firm claim to the riches and territory which the two had lavishly described. The lure of rumored gold was so strong that Coronado and the viceroy invested more than four million dollars in his expedition, an astronomical sum in 1540.

Coronado was only thirty years old. He led several hundred soldiers, priests, Indians, and more than 1,500 animals in search of the seven cities of Cibola. The fabled sites proved to be the multi-storied adobe pueblos in New Mexico. Coronado's expedition ranged all the way from Kansas to the Grand Canyon, but he was an absolute failure at treasure hunting. He crossed the Llano Estacado in the spring of 1591, discovered Palo Duro Canyon, encountered the Plains Indians, and crossed the northwest corner of the Panhandle on his return. He returned to Mexico City, broken and bitterly disappointed. Burned by the outlandish investment, the administration of New Spain proceeded to ignore Texas for more than a century.

The next foreign expeditionary force into Texas was launched not by Spain but by France. In January 1685, three tiny ships approached the middle of the Texas coast. The three, *L'Aimable*, *La Belle*, and *Le Joly*, were under the command of the famous French explorer, René Robert Cavalier, Sieur de La Salle.

In the court at Versailles, La Salle was a hero of the stature of Neal Armstrong, the astronaut who, not quite three centuries later, walked on the moon. In North America, La Salle had

Lifting a hull member from La Salle's ship, La Belle

Exposed hull members, La Salle's ship, La Belle

the king, the 51-footer was the smallest ship in the flotilla. La Salle found anchorage in one of our most beautiful estuaries, but the explorer and his entourage found the beginnings of French empire in Texas to be a sweltering, fever-ridden hellhole.

With La Salle was a companion and journalist, Henri Joutel, whose subsequent report was almost as astonishing as the memoir of Cabeza de Vaca. Leaving *La Belle* at anchor behind the protective barrier peninsula, La Salle set out on foot to find the mouth of the Mississippi, while colleagues began construction of a permanent settlement, Fort St. Louis. While La Salle was gone, men dying of thirst sought relief in his stores of brandy and became so impaired that they were unable to save *La Belle* when she ran aground and broke up in a violent winter storm.

In January 1687, La Salle set out again with seventeen men for Illinois, leaving twenty behind at Fort St. Louis. Only these remained of the 180 who had made landfall two years before. The rest had succumbed to illness and the hostility of the local Karankawa Indians.

The French hero La Salle did not survive. He was ambushed by his own men and his body was stripped and left to the animals somewhere in the post oak savannah between the Brazos and the Trinity rivers. Within a year, smallpox and the Karankawas finished off the inhabitants of Fort St. Louis. Spaniards burned what was left to the ground in 1689.

Although La Salle's second adventure in the New World was calamitous for him and for his country, it aroused the institutions of colonial new Spain and reverberated all the way back to the Spanish court. For the first time, Spaniards took serious steps to defend the huge northern frontier they believed to be theirs.

The first evidence of a renewed attentiveness in response to La Salle was Mission San Francisco de las Tejas, which failed primarily because of an epidemic of European diseases among the Indians. But the mission strategy, a unique Spanish collaboration between church and state, established almost forty settlements in Texas by the end of the eighteenth century. These

Above: *Twin belfries at Mission Concepción, San Antonio Missions National Historical Park*

Left: *Historic decorations at Mission Concepción, San Antonio Missions National Historical Park*

Above: *Bell tower at Mission Espada, San Antonio Missions National Historical Park*

Right: *Holy water font at Mission Espada, San Antonio Missions National Historical Park*

Altar statuary at Mission San Juan Capistrano, San Antonio Missions National Historical Park

ecclesiastical outposts were strategically placed over the years along a sweeping crescent from Mission San Francisco de la Tejas in the east to San Bernardo on the Rio Grande where all lands drained by the great river were claimed for the empire.

The scheme was humanitarian, evangelical, economic, and tactical all at once. In theory, it was a strong concept reflecting the institutional synthesis of religion and politics at the top. Each mission, sometimes guarded by a garrison of Spanish soldiers in a nearby presidio, was situated in the territory of one of the known groups of Texas Indians.

Priests were to recruit Indians as both laborers and parishioners and, in the process, convert them and make them Spanish subjects. Some of the native peoples came into the mission compounds to till the gardens, tend horses and cattle in Texas' first ranches, and help erect the structures themselves. Some even became Christians. The Spanish called them *reducidos* or "the reduced."

Often, though, and with brutal, unintended consequences, institutional practice did not live up to theory. Many of the primitive and innocent *reducidos* literally died off from demoralization or disease.

Nearly one hundred years later, inhabitants of the northernmost mission of Santa Cruz de San Sabá were massacred by Indians, provoking a massive show of force by the army of New Spain. The soldiers were turned back by Comanches and Taovayas at Spanish Fort. Their defeat permanently stalled the expansion of the Spanish empire in Texas.

To the south, near the headwaters of the San Antonio River, Franciscan priests had established the first of five missions in early 1718. Mission buildings stood for many years in Texas, but only those at San Antonio and El Paso made it into the nineteenth century in functional condition. Some of these structures became sites for important historic events and new communities; others simply fell into ruin and disappeared. Today their remains are among the most lovely and meaningful of our historic places.

Left: *Spear points, probably from Coronado's expedition, found in Crosby County*

Below: *Historic Espada aqueduct carried water from the San Antonio River to mission gardens*

Bronze cannon from La Salle's *ship,* La Belle

Not until the twentieth century were serious preservation efforts launched on their behalf. Some missions were saved by the Catholic church, by citizens like Adina de Zavala and Clara Driscoll who led efforts to preserve the Alamo, and by the federal government—initially as part of the Depression-era Works Progress Administration.

Today, the San Antonio missions—except for the Alamo—are administered by the National Park Service in a unique partnership among the state, local parishes, the San Antonio Conservation Society, and a group of supportive citizens known as Los Compadres. The Alamo, while owned by the state, is administered by the Daughters of the Republic of Texas, and the old church at Goliad (Mission Espiritu Santo) is in the stewardship of Texas Parks and Wildlife. Other survivors continue to be used as parish churches in a poignant and continuing observance of the tradition which first settled Texas.

To be present at a mass, a funeral, or a quinceañera at Espada, Ysleta, Capistrano, or any of the old mission chapels evokes an era of intense imperial competition and colonization. Being there is also a means of joining a cultural continuum that serenely inspires the character of Texas today.

*I*n perhaps the most inspiring archeological discovery of modern times in Texas, La Salle's ship *La Belle* was discovered lying in the mud bottom of Matagorda Bay by the Texas Historical Commission, 309 years after she went down. For almost a year, *La Belle* lay at the bottom of a huge dry pit within sight of the vast wetlands of Matagorda Peninsula, while a massive archeological excavation salvaged the ship and her contents. Viewing the wreck from the rim of the massive cofferdam was like peering down into an operating theater in which the patient of mythic origin lay.

But she was real.

La Belle was remarkably well preserved for she was covered with sand soon after she sank. Archeologists from the Commission recovered over 700,000 items from the wreck, including timbers, cannons, muskets, trade goods, rat skeletons, cockroach eggs, and human remains. Little is known about seven

Church at San Elizario

teenth-century sailing vessels, and this astounding discovery provides much needed knowledge about their design and construction. Displacing fifty to sixty tons, the tiny ship had three compartments for anchor rope storage, cargo, and the quarters of the crew.

The Spanish and French explorers who left these fascinating hints of their being were the astronauts of their age. They navigated unknown seas and walked an unknown land. Now, even as the study and preservation of La Belle continues, that triumph of human spirit and adventure is carried on in Texas as NASA looks past Earth's atmosphere to the moon and Mars and beyond.

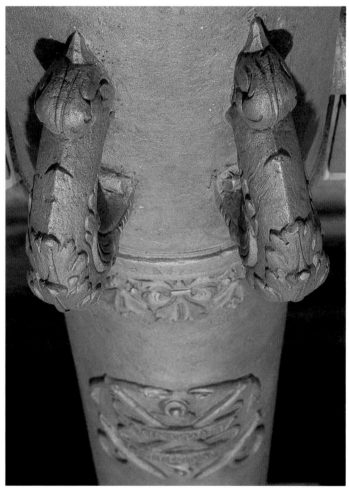

Dolphin detail from La Salle's ship, La Belle

Pages from Independence Convention journal, courtesy Dallas Historical Society

CHAPTER THREE

Backwoodsman, Empresarios, and Revolutionaries

My kids and I used to spend hours together walking along the shores of the Gulf Intracoastal Waterway at its intersection with the mouth of the Brazos River. The place is called Quintana, and today's busy barge canal cuts through the old town site where the first boatload of Stephen F. Austin's colonists landed in Texas. When you wade in the shallow water gently lapping up against the bank of the waterway, buttons, pieces of ceramics, and other early nineteenth-century artifacts occasionally wash up at your feet.

The colonists actually arrived at Quintana by mistake. They intended to meet Austin at the mouth of the Colorado, forty miles west. In the tradition of Cabeza de Vaca and La Salle, their schooner *Lively* foundered along the coast, and in the end, many gave up on Texas and returned to the United States.

Beach at Quintana, Brazoria County, where the first boatload of Stephen F. Austin's colonists landed

Other immigrants were more stubborn. Streaming through the woods all the way from Appalachia and beyond came a vanguard of frontiersmen and their families. They lived off the land and cherished the release and solitude—if not the danger—of life on the leading edge of the wilderness frontier. They were hardy and ferocious enough to survive Indian attacks along the way but too independent to tolerate the inevitable rules and regulations of more organized society.

The new waves of immigrants who pushed on through the forest and prairies to Texas were expatriate Americans. They risked their necks to start over as citizens of the young nation of Mexico, whose distant leaders and institutions were consumed with trying to solidify their freedom from Spain. The immigrant Texans would hack out a clearing in the deep woods for a home that was essentially a base camp. As hunters and subsistence farmers, they lived much as the Indians whom they displaced and fought did.

A few of these vernacular structures are left today in East Texas. In San Augustine, thanks to the unbelievable energy and dedication of a homegrown architect and preservationist named Raiford Stripling, the Milton Garrett house typifies that period. Built in 1826 along the highway of commerce called the Camino Real, the Garrett house is a primitive but hauntingly elegant log home. It is very small—eighteen by thirty feet—and very simple. But its squared logs and dovetail notching display fine craftsmanship. There is no ornamentation to speak of. At the time of its purchase from the Garrett family in 1920, it had never had a coat of paint.

*A*ustin's original 300 colonists in the Brazos and Colorado bottomlands probably lived in similar log cabins when they first arrived. They were a diverse lot: families and single men, slave-owners and adventurers, aristocrats and tradesmen. Some lived in lean-tos and some built mansions. The expansion of the North American frontier into Texas was as uncontrollable as a racing brush fire and, as these expatriate pioneers raced along with it, leaders in Mexico City grew increasingly concerned about the Americanization of the nation's neglected

Milton Garrett log home near San Augustine, built in 1826

northern province. On April 6, 1830, any further colonization of Mexican territory by nationals of neighboring countries was forbidden—meaning, of course, the United States. Ironically, the Spanish view of immigration across the Red and the Sabine rivers as illegal entry then is viewed in the same way along the Rio Grande today.

Mexico also cracked down on immigrant colonists already residing in Texas by dispatching army garrisons north of the Rio Grande, imposing new taxes, and generally making life difficult for the settlers—most of whom seemed not to mind being citizens of Mexico as long as they were left alone.

These settlers had become accustomed to self-government

The Alamo in the midst of modern San Antonio

though they were being ruled by a society deeply ingrained to conform. Any evidence of self-determination on the part of the citizens could only be interpreted by the Mexican leadership as insurrection, and it was this cultural disconnection that caused the leadership to make the most disastrous mistake in Mexican history, bringing its status as the leading power in the Americas to an end.

The first shots of the Texas revolution were fired at Gonzales in the fall of 1835 by a motley band of Texans who had meant to stop the Mexican government from confiscating a small cannon that the colony had been issued for use against the Indians. More out of confusion than anything else, the Mexican troops retreated. This emboldened the Texans to march on San Antonio, and their confidence increased when they took possession of Goliad. On December 10, 1835, the Mexican garrison of more than 1,100 troops at San Antonio surrendered and turned over the old Alamo mission to a ragtag band of 350 Texans.

Santa Anna, who had come to power in Mexico with the support of the Texans, was not remotely amused at their insurrection. In a remarkable logistical achievement, the Mexican chief of state led an army of 2,000 from Mexico City to San Antonio in just two months. Hunkered down inside the Alamo, the 189 defenders fit no uniform description. Many had joined the Texas army to get free Texas land; others were scions of Hispanic families who had prospered in Texas for generations; others, like Davy Crockett and Jim Bowie, were speculators in commerce and seekers of adventure.

During Santa Anna's siege of the Alamo, a revolutionary convention of Texans declared independence at Washington-on-the-Brazos on March 2, 1836. But the Alamo fell just four days later, and the Mexican army executed a captured garrison of 400 men at Goliad, while settlers-turned-war-refugees fled for the Sabine River in the chaotic exodus called the Runaway Scrape.

General Sam Houston, a man of myth and lore as big as Texas herself, commanded what was left of the Texas army. He was a protégé of American President Andrew Jackson and had served as governor of Tennessee. Following a disastrous marriage, he quit his office and fled to the wilderness of Texas, living for several years among Indians who called him Big Drunk.

After receiving word of the fall of the Alamo, Houston ordered a strategic retreat. Dividing his forces, Santa Anna pursued Houston's retreating army to a swampy peninsula in Galveston Bay between Buffalo Bayou and the San Jacinto River and prepared to bring the rebellion to an end.

On the afternoon of April 21, Sam Houston held a council of war with his officers. The decision was made to attack immediately. Frustrated by the long, humiliating retreat, the Texans fell on the Mexican army during siesta and in a rage of bloodletting avenged the Alamo and Goliad. Texas was an independent nation.

*T*exas prospered slowly during the years of the Republic and the first years of statehood. Many people continued to live in rough log houses, especially in outlying areas where wood was plentiful. Clearing land for fields provided timber for building—thus the labor of cutting trees served a dual function. In more urban areas, however, lumber mills and imported building materials enabled construction of dwellings in the fashionable Greek Revival style. And in the countryside, large houses became the vogue of plantation owners in the 1840s and 1850s.

In contrast to the isolation of the self-sufficient homesteads, towns like San Augustine, Nacogdoches, San Antonio, and Galveston had a varied social life and access to a variety of goods and services. Brazoria County was the center of the Texas coastal plantation culture. Sugar and cotton were grown on a large scale in the traditional slave-holding plantation system. Dependent on an involuntary work force, the plantations withered after Emancipation. Ruins of a few large sugar mills remain, and some big houses still stand. But for the most part, that era's noisy beehives of activity are now overgrown by the lush vegetation of the coast.

*T*oday, the hallowed places of the Texas Revolution are well taken care of. Washington-on-the-Brazos is a state park supported by an association of citizens from Brenham, Navasota, and beyond. Blinn College operates the Star of the Republic of Texas Museum on the site, and this strong partnership is responsible for recent improvements at the park: They include a full interpretation of the old town site, restoration of the nineteenth-century Barrington farm with a living history program, and a modern visitor center which will house the manuscript journal of Convention proceedings. This treasured document has been made available to the citizens of Texas by the Summerlee Foundation and the Dallas Historical Society.

In downtown San Antonio, the old Alamo mission was abandoned after the battle and at one time was reduced to the storage of hay. After prodding by the Daughters of the Republic of Texas, the site was acquired by the state of Texas in 1905. At that time, the Legislature directed that the property be placed

Matthew Cartwright house in San Augustine built in 1839, still in Cartwright family ownership

Sugar mill ruins and big house at Varner-Hogg Plantation State Historical Park, near West Columbia

Archeological excavations at Abner Jackson Plantation, Lake Jackson

in the custody of the Daughters, and, in the hands of that organization, it remains Texas' best-known icon, despite continuing controversies surrounding its stewardship and presentation.

In San Augustine and other towns, examples of antebellum Texas architecture have been preserved. Among them is the lovely Cartwright home. Still in the family of Matthew Cartwright, who at the time of his death in 1870 owned one million acres of Texas land, the house was designed and built by master builder San Augustine Phelps and later restored by Raiford Stripling. Its heavy pediments and Doric columns capture the creative balance of grandeur and restraint that characterizes the Greek Revival period.

The extremely destructive climate and the relatively short duration of the period have reduced Gulf Coast plantation architecture to a few remnants. Donated to the state by philanthropist Ima Hogg in 1958 and administered by the Texas Parks and Wildlife Department, Varner-Hogg Plantation State Historical Park typifies the plantation way of life. Under the huge oaks of the Brazos bottomlands, ruins of the old sugar mills can still be seen, along with an old family cemetery. In recent years, residents of the West Columbia area have worked closely with Parks and Wildlife staff to interpret the story previously untold of African-American life in Texas during the years of bondage and the struggles and contributions of freedmen following Reconstruction.

Just a few miles away, another example of plantation architecture hangs by a thread. The Levi Jordan house was built by one of Brazoria County's most successful planters in 1854. Made of heart pine imported from Florida and erected by crews drawn from Jordan's slaves, the old house stands today as one of the few specimens of that era in coastal Texas. And in nearby Lake Jackson, on the banks of the lake which bears his name, the ruins of Abner Jackson's plantation site have been preserved and studied by the successive field schools of the Texas Archeological Society.

San Jacinto Monument rises 570 feet in San Jacinto Battleground State Historical Park

At San Jacinto, the marshy prairie where Texas won her independence is looked after by various interests, all bound together by their commitment to the site. In 1936, on the occasion of the centennial of the battle, civic leaders initiated efforts to erect a limestone obelisk and an adjacent reflecting pool in the colossal style of the Washington Monument. Later, after World War II, a resting place was prepared at San Jacinto for the retired battleship, USS *Texas*. These elements and the battlefield today comprise the San Jacinto Battleground State Historical Park. In the park, a private organization, the San Jacinto Museum Association, maintains an extensive collection of important Texas documents and artifacts, many of which are on display in the monument itself.

Texas Parks and Wildlife is currently directing extensive restoration of the huge shrine which is expected to be completed by the end of the century. The task of protecting both the physical elements and the story itself remains a challenge in this place where a buckskin army overthrew Mexican rule; but Hispanic culture is even more a part of Texas today than it was at that time.

Main house of Levi Jordan Plantation, near Brazoria

The highest of the four Medicine Mounds, near Quanah in Hardeman County

CHAPTER FOUR

Indian Wars

Out on the rolling plains near the Pease River is a place called Medicine Mounds. Four smoothly rounded hillocks rise up out of the Texas veldt and stand like primordial mon uments against the sky in illusionary scale. At a distance the sentinel peaks look much larger than they really are. To the Comanches, this was magical and sacred ground, inhabited by spirits of great power and benevolence. Because Comanches were entirely nomadic, there is very little physical evidence of them on the Texas landscape, but here it is possible to achieve some sense of their presence and their place in the history of Texas.

Yet another nation of immigrants, the Comanches were not even present in Texas when the Spanish arrived in the sixteenth century. In fact, it was not until Juan de Oñate marched northward from Mexico, named the region New Mexico, and unin

Cairn of unknown origin, Foard County

tentionally delivered horses to the Apaches that conditions enabled Comanche dominion to occur.

In the wake of Oñate's great *entrada*, mission settlements were established at the indigenous pueblos, and the Indians were trained to tend the animals. As a direct result of these frontier remudas, the utilization of horses was passed to the Native Americans. While the acquisition of the horse enabled the Apaches to meet the Europeans on more equal terms, it turned another struggling people from the eastern slope of the Rockies into one of the most formidable forces of mounted tribal warriors since the rule of other plains by the marauders of Genghis Khan.

By the beginning of the eighteenth century, 200 years after the first Spaniards arrived in Texas, bands of the tribe that other Indians called the Snake People and the Spanish called Komantcia, or Comanche, rode into Texas. They called themselves the Human Beings—as most indigenous peoples did in

Moon over Medicine Mounds

Plains Apache tipi rings, Armstrong County

their own tongues—and their only concept of land ownership was as a right to be gained or lost in combat. The Comanches pushed the fierce Apaches all the way out of the plains into mountainous strongholds in Arizona and New Mexico.

Comanches assumed command of the southern Great Plains, as they followed the largest concentration of big game animals anywhere on the earth—the southern bison. The southern buffalo herd was then so vast that European travelers could scarcely describe it, and the animals' continuous migration on the plains of Texas in search of water and grass was perfectly suited to the Comanches and their horse culture; in fact, the Comanches became almost completely dependent on the buffalo commissary for material and spiritual sustenance. Loosely allied with the Kiowas, Kiowa-Apaches, and Southern Cheyennes, for more than a century the Comanches were absolute rulers of the plains and plateaus of Texas.

The "Indian Problem" which had plagued Spain and Mexico and limited settlement in all regions of Texas became even more troublesome after Texas won independence from Mexico. The Comanches and other hostile tribes were aggressive, and more and more settlers were moving into the buffalo range. Just one month after San Jacinto, a band of Comanches killed several settlers and kidnapped their children, including a nine-year-old girl named Cynthia Ann Parker. She grew up with her captors following the buffalo and became a Comanche in all ways except her blood.

Soon, Sam Houston, the hero of San Jacinto, became president of the Republic, and having lived among the Indians, he understood their ways. His attempts to negotiate with them were seen by the settlers as soft-headed, and when he was succeeded by Mirabeau B. Lamar, the fledgling government went after the Indian tribes with a vengeance.

In 1846, as Texas was annexed into the Union, responsibility for dealing with the Indians ostensibly passed to the federal government, but the U.S. Army did not yet include true cavalry and thus lacked the mobility to be effective against what were essentially skillful mounted guerrillas. This impotence was com-

Stone ruins at Fort Chadbourne, Coke County

pounded by the fact that Washington would only allow the soldiers to engage the Indians when they were attacked.

As the War between the States drew federal troops back east, the Army abandoned a line of fortifications that had been established during the California gold rush to guard wagon trains and postal routes. Frontier settlements naturally grew up around them, and now, with the federal troops removed, Comanches and Kiowas raided with virtual impunity. The frontier retreated and the Civil War in Texas was primarily an Indian war.

During this period a loosely organized but deadly paramilitary home guard which came to be known as the Texas Rangers protected the northern and western frontier. In December 1860, rangers under the command of Major Sul Ross attacked a band of Comanches on a bend of the Pease River just south of the Medicine Mounds. The Texans had come to avenge a devastating Comanche raid through the Brazos valley. A scout and

53

Restored headquarters and ruins of commanding officer's quarters, Fort McKavett State Historical Park, Menard County

Restored hospital at Fort Richardson State Historical Park, near Jacksboro

future pioneering cattle baron named Charles Goodnight saw the blue eyes of one woman and saved her life. It was Cynthia Ann Parker. She and her infant daughter Topsannah were returned to their relatives; at one point they were presented to the state convention in Austin considering Texas' secession from the United States. Topsannah soon died of illness, and in 1864, Cynthia Ann, who could never adjust to her life's second captivity, died essentially of a broken heart. She also had two sons. The eldest of these, who would be known by the Texans as Quanah Parker, came of age on the rolling plains guarded by the mystery of Medicine Mounds. He was the last great chief of the Comanches.

After Appomatox, federal troops were again sent to Texas to restore order and enforce new requirements that Texas Indians be placed on reservations in Oklahoma. This policy, of course, provided the Indians with federally guaranteed sanctuaries to which they could return safely, infuriating the Texans.

Under intense pressure from Texas, Congress directed the Army to bolster the line of forts along the frontier. Along with Fort McKavett and Fort Davis, which had been established before the war, and Fort Clark on the Rio Grande, garrisons were placed at Fort Griffin near Albany, Fort Richardson at Jacksboro, and Fort Concho at San Angelo.

Troops at these outposts included a new fighting force of African Americans whom the Indians called Buffalo Soldiers. Two cavalry and infantry regiments of black enlisted men served in Texas from 1866 to the early 1890s and saw service throughout the Texas frontier. Their valiant service on the frontier, which garnered nineteen Congressional Medals of Honor, went largely unrecognized until recent times.

In the 1867 Treaty of Medicine Lodge, the federal government promised that all bison hunting south of the Arkansas River would be reserved for Native Americans. But with the certain knowledge that the Comanches would never be defeated as long as the buffalo were plentiful, the army looked the other way. In spite of the treaty, the federal government chose not to stop

Fort Chadbourne, Coke County

Comanche petroglyphs, near Post

the greatest slaughter of wild animals in human history and the elimination of the Comanche commissary.

The center of the carnage was at Fort Griffin. The influx of buffalo hunters, skinners, and traders helped turn the neighboring town in the Brazos River bottom into one of the most notoriously lawless frontier outposts in the west. During its short unruly existence, the town of Fort Griffin attracted the likes of Pat Garrett, Doc Holliday, and Wyatt Earp. The famed Conrad's Store was the primary supplier for both the army and the hunters and sold hundreds of the preferred Sharps buffalo rifles to the hunters.

As the great hunt intensified, rotting carcasses and huge piles of bones began to appear all across the plains. In Austin, the Legislature considered affording the bison herd some protection. The effort might well have been successful had not General Phillip Henry Sheridan been allowed to address a joint session and plead that only extermination of the buffalo would starve the Indians into submission: "Then your prairies can be covered with speckled cattle, and the festive cowboy, who follows the hunter as a second forerunner of advanced civilization."

But not just yet. In the summer of 1871, sick and crazed by the annihilation of their sustenance, a group of Kiowas and Comanches led by the warrior Satanta set out from the reservation in Oklahoma on a killing spree. Satanta's bloody work so affected General William T. Sherman that the military strategy in Texas shifted to the offensive.

Sherman had Satanta and a younger warrior arrested on the reservation and they were convicted of murder in a Texas court. Incredibly, they were set free by federal authorities in negotiation with the Indians. Satanta quickly killed again and was once more put in prison, where he leaped from a second-story window to his death.

Now it was left to Quanah Parker to make the last stand. The son of Cynthia Ann had long since proved himself as a warrior, and in the summer of 1874, he and other chiefs of the last Plains Indian tribes remaining in Texas came together. Along with his Comanches were Kiowas, Kiowa-Apaches, Southern Cheyennes, and Arapahos. On June 27, several hundred warriors struck a buffalo hunters' camp on the Canadian River known as Adobe Walls. Blessed with astounding luck and armed with the accurate and long-range big Sharps rifles, twenty-eight hunters—one of whom was Bat Masterson—repelled the attack and shattered the confederacy. One Indian was shot off his horse at an incredible distance of 1,500 yards.

Within weeks, Colonel Ranald Mackenzie was ordered to pacify the Southern Plains for once and for all. In September 1874, Mackenzie learned that Quanah and his forces were camped on the floor of Palo Duro Canyon. Reaching the edge of the magnificent gorge on September 28, the soldiers crept and skidded with their horses down the sheer canyon walls and caught the Indians by surprise. Although only four warriors were killed and the rest escaped, Mackenzie destroyed all their tipis and supplies, then drove 1,400 horses back to his supply base and ordered them shot.

The following summer, having lost the horse which had come

JA buffalo from Charlie Goodnight's herd

Restored 1870s Fort Brown buildings, University of Texas at Brownsville-Texas Southmost College, Brownsville

Texas Buffalo Soldiers encampment at Guadalupe Mountains National Park

to define them and the buffalo which had sustained them, Quanah Parker and the remaining Comanches surrendered at Fort Sill, in southern Oklahoma.

*T*oday the story of the Buffalo Soldiers is told at each of the old frontier forts. Fort McKavett, Fort Griffin, and Fort Richardson are units of the Texas State Park System. Fort Concho is protected and managed by a non-profit organization. Fort Clark is a subdivision of Clarksville and Fort Davis is a National Historic Site.

Charles Goodnight, the scout who had saved the life of Cynthia Ann Parker along the Pease River, became the friend of her son. Goodnight turned the floor of Palo Duro Canyon into the JA, the Panhandle's first great cattle ranch. The legendary cattle baron decreed that a herd of buffalo would be protected in the canyon and their descendants graze there to this day.

Cavalry Trooper, Texas Buffalo Soldiers

Today's Texas cowboy

CHAPTER FIVE

Ranching Heritage

As the last mountains of buffalo hides were shipped back east where they were used for the heavy coats of the fashionable, the Plains Indians coped with reservation life and struggled to maintain their cultures. This sad and violent passage opened the plains to the cowboys and settlers and the one economic activity most closely tied to the identity of Texas and Texans. As if our own culture had been branded, the impact of the cattle-raising enterprise is more indelible than any other influence in terms of how we see ourselves and how others, in turn, have seen us.

During the late nineteenth century, in the time of Charles Goodnight and others, the distinctiveness and charm of ranching became widely appreciated for the first time, though its foundation, technology, and way of life had begun in Mexico two centuries earlier.

The first significant numbers of cattle and horses came to Texas with the Spanish expeditions sent north in response to the fears kindled by the French intrusion of La Salle. Many animals strayed or escaped into the wilderness; they were called *mesteños*, from which the word mustang was derived. These feral animals bred prolifically and formed the basis for the development of ranching in the eighteenth century.

The first ranches in Texas were associated with the missions, and the word "ranch" itself is derived from the Spanish *rancho*. In spite of the extreme difficulties presented by hostile Indians and the scant labor available to the priests, the mission ranches became rather extensive. The herds of Rancho de las Cabras—the remains of which are managed in Wilson County by the National Park Service as part of the San Antonio Missions National Historical Park—at one time included more than 500 horses, 1,000 sheep, 1,000 cattle, and numerous pigs, mules, and burros.

Rancho de las Cabras was the supply system for Mission Espada, and by the time of the American Revolution in 1776, over 3,000 head of cattle ran wild in its vicinity. Using inefficient tools and technology that had been employed in Mexico and Spain for hundreds of years, the missionaries were unable to brand more than a tiny percentage of their annual calf production. The offspring of the missionaries' unbranded cattle more closely resembled wildlife in their behavior than domestic animals, and the roundups by which they were captured and driven to market established the premise of ranching development in the following century.

During this period, ranches not affiliated with the missions spread northward through Mexico to the Rio Grande plains. The roundup and trailing of wild cattle to Coahuila and Louisiana was a source of conflict between settlers and the missions that claimed all the animals. This tension persisted until the early nineteenth century when expatriates from the United States entered the picture. The Spanish saddle, the lariat, the chaps, the bandana, the mustang and bronco, and the roundup itself were integral to the management and romance of the cattle industry in Texas, and it would be impossible to imagine ranching without them today.

Courtyard, main house, King Ranch

Main house, King Ranch

Tiffany windows in main house, King Ranch

Old horse barn, King Ranch

A century after the first ranchos were established in South Texas, Richard King, a riverboat pilot who was born in New York City, purchased from Juan Mendiola the Rincon de Santa Gertrudis, an original Spanish land grant of 15,500 acres. It became the most famous ranch in the world. During the early years of the ranch, King struggled to keep it together and expanded it by trading cattle for lumber to build fences. He carried on an almost continuous war with bandits and rustlers who took advantage of the disputed Nueces Strip claimed by both Texas and Mexico, and he transported whole villages of *campesinos* from Mexico to provide labor. These vaqueros came to be known as *Kineños* or King's men, and many of their descendants remain on the ranch as employees today.

In 1869, the famous "Running W" was registered by Richard King as the official brand of the ranch, and in time it appeared on the hides of stock grazing on more than one and a quarter million acres in eight South Texas counties.

Upon King's death in 1885, his widow asked their lawyer Robert Justus Kleberg to manage the ranch, and Kleberg later married their daughter Alice. The Kleberg family has dominated the ranch through the years and overseen its greatest achievements: development of measures to eradicate fever-bearing ticks, the founding of two railroads and the city of Kingsville, and development of one of the most successful breeds of cattle in the world, the Santa Gertrudis.

Today, King Ranch operations are diversified and spread throughout the world. Perhaps the Ranch's most enduring characteristic is the determination its leadership has shown throughout its history to maintain the legacy of one of Texas' most important places. Not only are its historic structures, including the grand old main house and commissary, maintained with numerous other physical artifacts of its remarkable era, but traditional practices of the past, such as the graceful *formando* by which horses are gathered for work in the morning, are faithfully carried on every day of the year.

The origins of the myths and customs of ranching in Texas are firmly rooted in the land between the Nueces and Rio Grande. That tradition is carried on in great ranches which bear the name of King, Kenedy, Kleberg, Armstrong, Yturria, Ysaguerre, Guerra, and Garcia, though opportunities and pressures of settlement soon lured the cowmen onward to the last open ranges of the Trans-Pecos and northern plains.

One of the most unique ranching entrepreneurs who moved west was Milton Faver. Don Melitón, as he came to be called, arrived in Presidio County on the eve of the Civil War and created a successful cattle operation by erecting a series of fortified ranches on the locations of natural springs. From behind thick adobe walls, he was able to defend his family and his vaqueros, as they ventured out to round up and brand wild cattle and trade with freighters in huge *carretas* moving back and forth from Indianola to Chihuahua City on the Old Chihuahua Trail. Faver irrigated peaches, made brandy, and sold beef to the garrison at Fort Davis; he became the largest rancher in Presidio County by 1880.

Dipping vat at King Ranch

Working chute at King Ranch

Ruins of ranch worker's house at Milton Favor's El Fortín de Cibolo, on Cibolo Creek Ranch, Presidio County

Barn at Four Sixes Ranch, near Guthrie, King County

Headquarters of Four Sixes Ranch, built in 1917 near Guthrie, King County

After the Civil War, driving large numbers of over-abundant Texas cattle became the primary means of getting them to new pastures or to market. Charles Goodnight and his partner Oliver Loving took a herd up to Colorado through New Mexico in 1866 and pioneered the trail which came to bear their names. They crossed the dry and pitiless desert of the Trans-Pecos to avoid Comanches and Kiowas, but the route exposed them to danger from Apaches in the Guadalupe Mountains; Loving died as the result of wounds suffered in one Indian fight. One hundred and twenty years later, their great but ultimately tragic adventure provided the inspiration for Larry McMurtry's epic Texas novel *Lonesome Dove.*

Texans took on that kind of hardship and risk because the cattle drives were at first fantastically profitable. In 1867, when the railroad reached Abilene, Kansas, the route of choice became the trail blazed across the Red River and through Indian Territory by a part-Cherokee trader named Jesse Chisholm. By 1876, when the defeat of the nomadic buffalo-hunting tribes had opened the plains to more railheads and concentrated settlement, the western trail to Ogallala and Dodge City, Kansas, was the drovers' principal route.

Though the period of the cattle drives left an enduring imprint on American myth and culture, the business practice lasted little more than a decade.

Using their proceeds from the drives, their expertise at rounding up unbranded "mavericks," and capital from England, Scotland, and eastern United States, Goodnight and others established great corporate ranches on the plains. Goodnight and an Irishman named John A. Adair formed a partnership and established the JA Ranch in Palo Duro Canyon in 1877. Cross-breeding Herefords and longhorns, Goodnight expanded his herd to 40,000 head, and eventually the JA encompassed more than 700,000 acres. In 1889, the partnership ended, and Goodnight settled on a smaller ranch whose headquarters were in the village named after him. The heirs of Adair remain on the JA today and have maintained his famous buffalo herd along with many of the original ranch structures.

Charles Goodnight home, near his namesake town in Armstrong County

Corner of a reconstructed dug-out at the Ranching Heritage Center of the Museum of Texas Tech University, Lubbock

During the last two decades of the nineteenth century, other great ranches were established on the plains, including the Four Sixes of Burk Burnett, the Matador, the Pitchfork, and the XIT. These huge spreads brought a new dimension to the cattle industry with managers and boards of directors on the East Coast or across the Atlantic.

And the new breed was innovative. Although the romance of the open range defines many people's perceptions of Texas ranching in the nineteenth century, fencing came first to South Texas, and a ruinous drought in the early 1880s reinforced the sensible practice in the Trans-Pecos and Panhandle. Texas ranches gained a new look: windmills and barbed wire.

*I*n 1884, Texas cattle barons successfully petitioned Congress to establish a National Cattle Trail that was six miles wide and stretched to Canada. But settlement, railroads, and Great Plains farming soon made that grand scheme an almost quaint memory. Texas ranching today has changed vastly. Early ranches in West Texas, built on free grass and proving up valuable sections, evolved into owned or leased properties, with fences, windmills, line camps, and other innovations, which required capital investment. Today, in contrast to the frontier animus between farmers and ranchers, grazing operations are often combined with cultivation of feed crops, especially hay. And on the Edwards Plateau and in the Trans-Pecos, as erratic climate and too-frequent overstocking thinned out the once limitless prairies, vast stretches of Texas ranching territory became better suited to herds of sheep and Spanish and mohair goats. But the image of the visionary cattlemen is forever seared into the Texas psyche.

San Augustín Plaza of Laredo and the historic San Augustín Church, founded in 1760

CHAPTER SIX

Melting Pot

The lure was always the land and the opportunity. Though the stirrings of revolution and enlightenment pulsed throughout the world during Texas' formative years, most who came here did so simply for the chance to work a piece of ground and to make a better life for themselves and their families. This burning impulse is the common bond in an otherwise unusually variegated pattern of human settlement. Its diversity is reflected in a habitat that both accommodates it and celebrates it.

In the next generation, less than fifty years from now, the population of Texas will double. At that time, if demographic projections are accurate, the majority of Texans will be of Hispanic and African-American descent, and Texans of northern European ancestry will be in the minority. This coming sea change in the ethnicity of our population will have impact on every single one of us and will provide us with a rich and intense experience. Profound though this approaching metamorphosis promises to be, the history of Texas is replete with such compelling encounters of powerful cultural forces, and their blending is the richest aspect of our history.

*F*rom the beginning, the most persistent and indelible braid in the fabric has been Hispanic. People from Mexico built the first towns: Nacogdoches in 1716, San Antonio in 1718, La Bahía (Goliad) in 1749, and Laredo in 1755. Gracefully centered by the plaza and church of San Augustín, Laredo was the last town established in the Spanish province of Nuevo Santander by José de Escandón. The rationale for this new settlement, in the minds of the powers in Mexico City, was to pacify an untamed strip of wilderness between civilization in Mexico and the southern border of Texas, which they considered to be the Nueces. Escandón, sometimes called the father of the Rio Grande Valley, founded twenty-four settlements—all but two of them south of the Rio Grande. Still, the initiative established a beachhead for immigration and created a sector which continued to develop as stockmen moved their herds of sheep, cattle, and goats across the river. This northward flow of Mexican pioneers set the cultural pattern for the borderlands and inspired the art, architecture, and customs of their people.

Since at least the 1840s, the tiny community of Los Ebanos—named for a grove of ebony trees—has been a popular crossing of the Rio Grande. A continuously operating hand-pulled ferry was established in 1950 and remains the only officially recognized hand-pulled ferry on the U.S. border. At the end of the eighteenth century, residents along the river far outnumbered those dispersed throughout the rest of Texas. Both sides of the river were then in Mexico and remained so through the Texas revolution and through the granting of statehood, when the Mexican War established the Rio Grande as a permanent border.

In San Ygnacio, another Rio Grande settlement founded about 1830, Jesus Treviño built the first part of what became Fort Treviño. Inhabitants of the area relied on it through the mid-nineteenth century for protection against the raids by

Los Ebanos ferry at an ancient crossing of the Rio Grande

Gun port at Rancho San Francisco, near San Ygnacio

Comanches and Apaches. The large mesquite doors and loop-holes provided security for those besieged inside. Ranch architecture in the community also addressed this need. Built near San Ygnacio about 1840, Rancho San Francisco had its own gunports within the stout walls.

After independence was won at San Jacinto, the fledgling government of the Republic continued the Hispanic strategy of making land grants to empresarios for settlement. Thus, in 1842 Henri Castro, a Frenchman and Sam Houston's consul general in Paris, contracted with the Republic to settle 600 families in Texas. These German-speaking settlers were recruited from another disputed border region, the Alsace in France, and traces of their heritage have been among the most persistent in the advance of Texan cultures.

During its first year of existence, Castro's colony, west of San Antonio along the Medina River, grew to more than 2,000 settlers, though it was beset by Indians, cholera, and drought. The town of Castroville, which came to be known as "Little Alsace," was laid out like a European village; each lot in the community was surrounded by an individual farming plot. Today, ninety-seven historic buildings have been preserved in the old city, and many have been continuously occupied by businesses and residents since the Alsatian community's earliest days.

Local legend has it that the bathhouse in the courtyard of what later would become the Landmark Inn State Historical Park was the only improved bathing facility between San Antonio and Eagle Pass. The founder of this ethnic stronghold in Texas is said to have been more like Stephen F. Austin than any of the other empresarios. Castro invested his own money for the welfare of his colonists and was by all accounts an educated, just, and caring man. His maps of the land grant were circulated widely across the Atlantic and helped stimulate the interests of other Europeans in Texas.

One empresario during early statehood who bore little resemblance to Austin or Castro was the German Prince Carl of Solms-Braunfels. The first German immigrants had

Rancho San Francisco

Thick walls of the interior of Treviño Fort, San Ygnacio

1830s wall of Treviño Fort, San Ygnacio

joined Austin's colony in Central Texas a decade earlier, and a group of minor German nobles, including Prince Carl, organized a society to facilitate the movement of settlers to Texas. The society believed their project would ease overpopulation at home while bringing them enhanced status and profits.

The Adelsverein, as the society was called, was an utter business failure, and though it managed to land more than 7,000 German settlers on the shores of Texas between 1844 and 1847, colonization was difficult and hazardous for the immigrants. Many of the new Texans perished trying to make their way to the colony from the port of Indianola.

The prince failed to provide adequately for their arrival and had not even legally secured the lands they had been promised. Worse still, all the port's teamsters had gone south with their mules to haul freight in the Mexican War. The Germans' walk from Indianola to the Hill Country stands as one of the harshest experiences in the settlement of Texas.

But the settlers eventually thrived in New Braunfels and in the limestone hills to the west. They made remarkable fences of heavy rock, built thick-walled homes of distinctive *fachwerk* architecture, and thanks to the Prince's successor, John Meusebach, became the only non-indigenous people to successfully negotiate and maintain a peace with the Comanches. New Braunfels and Fredericksburg became the western anchor of a German archipelago of enclaves stretching back east to the Trinity River, including the elegant King William district of San Antonio and numerous smaller communities with names like Schulenberg, Weimar, and Millheim. Today, in terms of national origin, descendants of German immigrants comprise the third largest segment of Texas' population. Their stoic dignity graces the verdant savannah of Central Texas in structures like St. Mary's Catholic Church at High Hill, one of the painted churches of Fayette County.

A few miles away from High Hill, the hamlet of Praha boasts another of these wonderful folk art chapels. St. Mary's Catholic Church was built by another group of middle Europeans who came to Texas in large numbers—the Czechs.

Bath house, Landmark Inn State Historical Park, Castroville

Anton Wulff house, 1870, home of the San Antonio Conservation Society, 107 King William Street, San Antonio

Home of Ferdinand Jacob Lindheimer, early Texas naturalist and newspaper publisher, New Braunfels

Steves Homestead, 1876, King William Street, San Antonio

Antioch Missionary Baptist Church, Houston

Sts. Cyril and Methodius Catholic Church, Dubina

St. Mary's Catholic Church, Praha

Immaculate Conception Catholic Church, Panna Maria

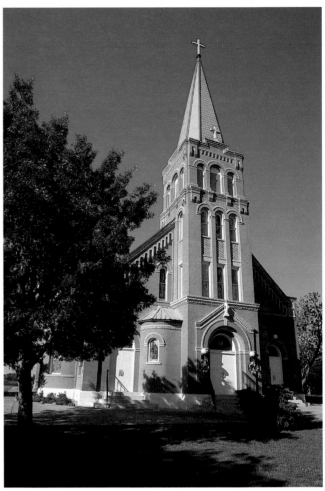

Holy Cross Catholic Church, Yorktown

Jack Yates family home, restored by the Heritage Society of Houston, Sam Houston Park

Portrait of Jack Yates in the living room of his home, Sam Houston Park, Houston

(Praha is Czech for Prague.) Although Fayette County is considered the center of the Czech population in Texas, these immigrants have spread northward into the blackland prairie due to its ideal farming conditions. For these Slavic people whose family structure was incredibly close knit, farming was more than a way of making money—it was an expression of the culture and a way of life. This tradition is so strong that Czech is still spoken across the blacklands today and two Texas newspapers are published in the Moravian dialect of the original settlers.

Catholicism played a role in bringing another group of immigrants from Silesia to Texas when a Polish priest, Father Leopold Moczygemba, influenced a hundred families to found the first permanent Polish settlement in the United States. Named Panna Maria (Virgin Mary) on Christmas Eve 1854, the first Polish Catholic church and school in America were established in Karnes County, and the parish is still active today.

*T*hough the ancient traditions of the European immigrants introduced a richness of culture that is today uniquely Texan, the vast majority of those who came were Anglo-Americans from the southern United States, and, before the Civil War, many brought with them another group of new Texans, most of whom did not come by choice: the African Americans.

The first black person in Texas was a slave. Estevanico and his master arrived on the beach in the same shipwreck that stranded Cabeza de Vaca. Like Cabeza de Vaca, Estevanico became a healer and traveled widely throughout Texas.

Most blacks who came before Emancipation were slaves, and although they numbered less than fifty in Texas at the beginning of the nineteenth century, by the 1861 outbreak of the Civil War in Texas, 182,000 people—thirty percent of the population—were slaves. The institution of slavery thrived in the Republic and early years of statehood, and laws were enacted that regulated slave behavior and imposed severe restrictions on free blacks—although treatment of slaves in Texas was probably no better or worse than in other parts of the South. Freedom

Dining room of Jack Yates home, Sam Houston Park, Houston

came to slaves in Texas only at the end of the Civil War, when Union General Gordon Granger arrived in Galveston and proclaimed all Texas slaves free on June 19, 1865, known ever since as Juneteenth.

Although slaves had been freed, blacks in Texas had a hard time during Reconstruction, building new lives and trying to work while subjected to prejudice, intimidation, and often violence. Nonetheless, many had developed skills on the plantations and used them to build homes for themselves in the rural areas and in the state's growing cities. This was also a time when many African Americans moved into Texas from other southern states, looking for work and opportunity.

Houston's Jack Yates was representative of the initiative that many black families throughout the state showed during the last quarter of the nineteenth century. A firm believer in the value of education and home ownership, Reverend Yates, a former slave, encouraged blacks to buy or build homes in Freedman's Town in Houston's Fourth Ward. Yates was the first pastor of the first black Baptist church in Houston, Antioch Missionary Baptist Church. He organized the Houston Academy, a school for black children, and led efforts to establish emancipation parks for the black people of Houston in 1872. His home has now been restored and made available to the public by the Heritage Society of Houston. Jack Yates High School was named for him in 1926.

Today in Texas, immigrants continue to come from Mexico, as always, but increasingly from other places as well, including Vietnam and other nations of Asia. In this context, the preservation of ethnic sites is more than a celebration of our origins. It is a measure of our commitment to our own humanity and to a future in Texas with room and opportunity for all.

Moody Mansion and Museum, Galveston

CHAPTER SEVEN

The Building Years

The fusion of cultures streaming into Texas during the nineteenth century created an alloy of human energy from which a modern, cosmopolitan society could be built. The crucible was on the wharves and streets of Galveston. Long thought to be the best natural port between Pensacola and Vera Cruz—due to its barrier of protection and lack of shoals and sand bars—antebellum Galveston evolved distinctly separate from the rest of Texas. The mix of languages in its hotels and shops and the licentious aroma of the seaport itself created a worldly and urbane aura that is still strong today. At one point, Galveston was second only to New York as a point of entry in this nation, and it was the leading edge of urban development in Texas.

Founded immediately after the War for Texas Independence, Galveston relied on steady streams of immigrants coming in and of cotton going out; it was the largest city in Texas by

1870. It had the first electric lights and telephone systems, and its newspaper, *The News*, is the oldest continuing daily in the state. In 1900 a mighty hurricane swamped Galveston, killing more than 6,000 people; it was the worst natural disaster in the history of the United States. But it could neither destroy Galveston's will to rebuild, nor its cosmopolitan sense of itself. That indomitable spirit is exemplified by the Moody family.

Though the flow of immigrants and seamen from foreign lands gave Galveston its unique character, cotton made the island city an engine for progress in the commercial development of Texas. And its driver was W. L. Moody. A classic Texas entrepreneur, Moody arrived in Galveston during the summer of 1866 and set himself up as a cotton broker. Knowing that a lack of organization in the trade would lead to financial disaster, he organized the Galveston Cotton Exchange in 1872.

From this beginning, Moody and his son built one of the great commercial empires of the United States—it included insurance, banking, hotels, and ranching. Like everything else in Galveston, the history of the Moodys is colorful and controversial. They created an empire that was both despised and admired, and through the years its spectrum of interests ranged from organized crime to organized charity. At one point, the Moody Foundation was the third largest philanthropic institution in the United States. In the last half of this century, the central figure of the vast Moody dominions was Mary Moody Northen, granddaughter of the founder. She embodied the elaborate eccentricities of the Moody heirs, but did more than any single person to preserve the history of the most distinctive city in Texas.

In 1964 Mary Moody Northen created her own private foundation to ensure, among other things, that the magnificent family mansion on Broadway would remain as a museum. A walk through the imposing structure provides a tangible sense of one of Texas' great dynasties and of the cotton empire upon which it was built.

Top: *Baronial dining room, Moody Mansion and Museum, Galveston*

Right: *Welcoming window at stair landing, Moody Mansion and Museum, Galveston*

93

*A*nother port community built on cotton lay several hundred miles north on the rim of ancient Caddo Lake. Founded in the 1840s, Jefferson was initially laid out with its main streets perpendicular to Big Cypress Bayou. Cleared for navigation, the murky, cypress-lined stream brought steamboats regularly up the Red River from Shreveport and New Orleans. By the end of the decade, Jefferson had become the leading inland port in Texas.

After the Civil War, a terrible fire destroyed most of Jefferson's commercial district, but as in the case of Galveston, it was rebuilt within a few years. Jefferson was by then the primary shipping point for cotton grown in a large area of Arkansas, Louisiana, and Texas. In 1870 it was Texas' sixth largest city and ranked second only to Galveston as a commercial and distribution center.

But during the last quarter of the nineteenth century, Jefferson's star faded. The Great Raft, a vast, centuries-old log-jam on the Red River, was cleared in 1873—and pulled the plug on the busy port on Big Cypress Bayou. The winding waterway back through the forest was no longer deep enough to support boat traffic, particularly during times of drought. Simultaneously, rail centers were established in Marshall and Dallas, and Jefferson was out of the loop.

Still, the elegant little town in the East Texas forest contains some of the finest nineteenth-century houses in the Southwest. Built by Benjamin Holland Epperson, a rail magnate and leader of the Whig Party in Texas, the House of the Seasons is an unusually sophisticated Italianate villa; the four seasons are figuratively portrayed in its cupola's stained glass. Today more than fifty of the homes and commercial buildings in Jefferson are privately preserved and listed in the National Register of Historic Places.

*A*bout the time that Jefferson began to flourish, a tiny settlement along the Rio Grande also was growing into a major Texas port. Roma was as far west as flatboats and steamers could navigate on the river, and it too became a principal port for the shipment of cotton.

House of the Seasons, Jefferson

Roma attracted the German master builder Heinrich
Portscheller, who designed and built many of its structures in a
distinct and highly developed brick architecture which reflects
both the fine craftsmanship of the region and a very elegant but
appropriate building style.

One of the earliest structures in Roma is the tower of Our
Lady of Refuge Church. Built in the mid-1850s, the tower has
been incorporated into the modern church. Roma's prosperity
as an inland port is evident in the Antonio Sáenz Residence,
the Nestor Sáenz Store, the so-called Ramírez Hospital, the
Noah Cox House, the Tino Ramírez Building, and the Manuel
Guerra Store and Residence, which has been restored by Texas
Parks and Wildlife in partnership with The Conservation Fund
and the Meadows Foundation.

In the late 1920s, several suspension bridges were built to
span the Rio Grande. The only one left connects Roma with
Mexico, and its 700-foot span is included among the city's
nationally recognized historic structures. Roma today is one of
the best-preserved town sites along the Rio Grande.

Opposite: *Last suspension bridge on the Rio Grande, Roma*

Top: *Manuel Guerra residence and store, 1884, Roma, restored by the Texas Parks and Wildlife Department, 1996*

Right: *Interior of Manuel Guerra store, Roma*

Old Southern Pacific Railroad Depot, now the Historic Brownsville Museum

All three towns refused to die; they are each enjoying a revival today as Texans and others embrace their heritage in history-laden communities. But the infrastructure that enabled them to prosper was desperately flawed. Getting around in early Texas was a nightmare—especially in the poorly-drained prairies and marshes around Galveston Bay, where mid-nineteenth-century commercial activity was centered. Building and maintaining a system of passable roads across the vast interior was highly problematic, and the streams were barely capable of supporting a reliable flow of riverboat traffic. For business leaders throughout the state, the railroads could not come soon enough.

The Republic's attempts to build railroads were all unsuccessful. Perhaps because statehood implied greater security, northern capital was finally secured by Sidney Sherman, William Marsh Rice, and a group of investors from Boston and Texas to build the Buffalo Bayou, Brazos and Colorado Railroad, which opened in 1853. This was the first working railroad in Texas, the second west of the Mississippi, and it became the oldest segment of the Southern Pacific.

Railroad construction was extremely difficult; it was in its infancy everywhere in the United States. Antebellum Texas had little investment capital, and financiers from Europe and the East Coast were reluctant to invest their money in so wild and untamed a place. The Legislature addressed this dilemma in 1854 by offering up to sixteen sections of land to the railroads for every mile of track laid; at that point building began in earnest. Partly because of that and subsequent massive transfers of land, in little more than a generation the public domain was exhausted.

In 1871 the U.S. Congress chartered the Texas and Pacific Railroad (T&P) to build trackage from Marshall, Texas, to San Diego, California, and authorized it to hook up with the Southern Pacific (SP) in Fort Yuma, Arizona. After false starts on both ends, the T&P arrived in Fort Worth in 1876, where construction stalled for want of funding until April 1880. The SP, however, had picked up steam and arrived in Yuma in September 1877. Taking advantage of the T&P right-of-way, the SP reached El Paso in May 1881.

Lacking a Texas charter, the SP hooked up with the Galveston, Houston and San Antonio Railroad (GH&SA) and laid track toward the pass at Sierra Blanca, racing with the revitalized T&P. The SP and GH&SA team reached Sierra Blanca on November 25, 1881, with the T&P still ten miles away. To normalize conflicts of rights-of-way and track ownership, two famous moguls of railroad lore, Collis P. Huntington (SP) and Jay Gould (T&P), agreed to share the track from Sierra Blanca westward. Meanwhile, the GH&SA had begun building track westward from San Antonio in 1881, and the two ends met at Langtry in January 1883, giving birth to the famed Southern Pacific Sunset Route.

No place in Texas was more profoundly affected by the evolution of a mature railway transportation system than Fort Worth, selected by the Texas and Pacific as its eastern terminus to California. The "City Where the West Begins" was already established as the jumping-off point for westbound stage lines, but the railroad took the city's development to a new level. Fort Worth flourished because it could now receive and ship large numbers of cattle. Later, major meat processors arrived and brought with them the stockyards and packing houses which established the identity of the city and created one of the most important industrial centers in the Southwest.

Today, the architectural expression of that great era is well-preserved. You can almost hear ghost cattle lowing in the Stockyards Historical District, which has become a major entertainment center, and sense the power of the railroads as the driving force of modernity in the restored passenger terminal of the Texas and Pacific. Fully nine blocks of the old downtown commercial district have been restored and thrive today through adaptive reuse.

Further east, in Dallas, the railroad transformed another small trading center into a commercial giant. The city became the primary intersection of railroad lines—north, south, east, and west. This provided wholesalers from throughout the United States with a strategic operational vantage point in Texas that continues to this day.

Cowtown moderne interior of the Texas & Pacific terminal, Fort Worth

Texas & Pacific terminal, Fort Worth

Interior of the Texas & Pacific terminal, Fort Worth

Fort Worth Stockyards entrance

Wilson Historical District, Dallas

Among the beneficiaries of Dallas' railroad boom were Frederick and Henrietta Wilson, who developed a spectacular neighborhood of Victorian residences today known as the Wilson Block, just east of downtown. With leadership from the Meadows Foundation, this collection of Victorian buildings is unmatched in the United States. All have been well restored and put to uses that protect their character and historical integrity, while ensuring their survival.

The tracks were slower to reach other parts of Texas, notably the Rio Grande Valley and the Panhandle. These areas were not well served until after the turn of the century. Nevertheless, the coming of the railroads and the distribution of real estate that facilitated them brought Texas out of the wilderness and into the twentieth century. By 1911 Texas possessed more railroad mileage than any other state, a position that it still holds today.

Fort Worth Stockyards pens

Abandoned mill race, Zedler's Mill, Luling

CHAPTER EIGHT

Boom
and
Bust

My wife's grandfather was a wildcatter. Like many others of his kind in the early part of the century, he followed the movements of the major oil companies and leased up land where he thought they were headed, sometimes successfully, sometimes not. He experienced wild swings in his fortunes, at times being wealthy and at times being broke. Whenever he drilled a new well, he would put on a new white linen suit, hoping to ruin it by bringing in a gusher.

Like the cowboys, Grandpa Wood and his peers contributed much more to Texas than the creation of wealth. Their resilience and panache are deeply imbedded in our collective psyche along with their unshaken belief in the next boom.

The most widespread industrial activity of Texas' formative years was milling. It is said that there are more streams in

Abandoned turbine, Zedler's Mill, Luling　　　　　　　*Turbine in mill pit, Landmark Inn State Historical Park, Castroville*

Texas called Mill Creek than by any other single name—an indication of how widespread this early business was. Grist-milling, in fact, was the largest industry in Texas until well after the Civil War. At its peak, there were several hundred water-powered, steam-powered, and even animal-driven mills throughout the state. Sadly, we have allowed almost all traces of them to disappear.

You can view the traces of an old mill on the Medina River in Castroville. Built by the partnership of a German and a Frenchman, the Haass-Quintle Mill was a custom operation to which local farmers brought their corn to be ground for household use. Haass and Quintle kept a share of the production for their efforts and operated a cotton gin on the side. By 1860, the mill was producing 9,000 bushels of corn meal and fifty bales of cotton annually.

By 1880, when milling reached its peak in Texas, the water wheel was supplemented by a steam engine and the production

Burton Cooperative Cotton Gin, Burton

of cornmeal, now primarily for market sale, reached a million pounds. Today, the framework of the old mill has been preserved as part of the Landmark Inn State Historical Park.

Many of these early mills were remarkable in their capacity, utilizing the water-driven mechanics to perform numerous useful functions beyond grinding corn. No one was better at getting the most out of a mill than Fritz Zedler. In 1884 Zedler and some partners bought an existing dam and gristmill on the San Marcos River at Luling. Zedler was a classic Texan of the day, having worked in the thirty years since his arrival at Indianola as a cowboy, freighter, Confederate soldier, and wheelwright. With no formal training he was essentially a self-taught engineer who leveraged the operation at Zedler's Mill to include a sawmill, cotton gin, electric power plant, and city water supply in addition to the gristmill. This ingenious and multifaceted operation, which typified the industry, ultimately included eleven buildings in the bend of the river and remained in service into the 1880s.

*T*exas' first real boom was in cotton, and the railroads were built to accommodate it. Prior to that transportation break-through, most farm families grew pretty much what they needed to sustain themselves and hauled corn or wheat to the local mill for grinding and sale. You could not eat cotton, and its bulkiness made shipping expensive. The trains changed all that.

Once the railroads came in, bringing products that could not be grown on the farm, the farmer had an increased need for cash which was most easily satisfied by growing cotton. The "Big Money Crop" took off. By 1890, Texas produced more than three million bales of cotton—up from less than a half million twenty years before. Cotton could be shipped long distances because it was not perishable, and it had a higher production value per acre than any grain.

Wherever cotton was grown, there was a gin. Eli Whitney's invention was so central to the efficient production of mar-ketable cotton that Stephen F. Austin offered land bounties to anyone who would build a gin. Even an animal-powered gin could raise the average worker's output from five pounds of cot-ton per day to fifty.

Jared E. Groce, one of Austin's Old Three Hundred, con-structed one of the earliest cotton gins in Texas on the Brazos River in Grimes County in 1825. Three years later there were four or five more in Austin's colony, and on the eve of the Civil War there were as many as 2,000 in Texas.

After the war, cotton exploded on the deep fertile soils of the Blackland Prairie—so much so that virtually all unbroken native sod completely disappeared, and production exceeded the cap-acity of the gins of the day. The tall-grass prairies that had lured settlers to Texas all but vanished behind barbed-wire fences and the moldboard plow.

For nearly a century, cotton ginning remained a labor-inten-sive process that focused on the primary function of cleaning the seed from the cotton. A Texan, Robert Munger of Mexia, revo-lutionized the industry with the development of "system gin-ning," which combined the functions of moving, cleaning, and baling cotton into one continuous, accelerated process.

Though Munger's improvements allowed the cotton bounty

Burton Cooperative Cotton Gin, Burton

Lummus cotton gins at Burton Cooperative Cotton Gin, Burton

Power generator, Burton Cooperative Cotton Gin, Burton

to continue to expand in Texas, system ginning was expensive and beyond the means of the average farmer. Most often, groups of farmers joined together in cooperatives that sold stock, built a modern gin, and performed other functions.

In this way, the Burton Farmers Gin Association constructed a two-story gin and cottonseed storage facility in Washington County in 1914. In a relationship typical of hundreds of similar operations across Texas, the Burton gin was the center of the community. Its function was the economic lifeblood and its whistles organized the day. The gin in Burton operated without interruption from 1914 to 1974. Although it is quiet now, it is a reminder of the many years in which cotton was the undisputed king.

About the time cotton really began to take off, silver was discovered near Milton Faver's domain in West Texas. John Spencer was a teamster who had taken up prospecting, and he found silver ore in the Chinati Mountains in 1880. A civilian employee of the Army, Spencer convinced the regimental commander at Fort Davis, Colonel William R. Shafter, and his fellow officers to join him in purchasing land around his claim. Lacking the expertise and money to initiate any kind of mining activity, the four men engaged an entrepreneur from San Francisco with experience in mining to move it forward. After satisfying himself that there was indeed silver on the property, Daniel Cook created the Presidio Mining Company of San Francisco with the four partners as stockholders and commenced large-scale operations in the spring of 1884.

There was a lot of silver. And as the mine grew, a community grew beside it and was named Shafter. At its peak, the town had over 4,000 inhabitants, mainly Mexican mineworkers and their families. The main street of Shafter had a Catholic church and school, a post office, saloons, and a jail. Although the surrounding countryside was stripped of all trees to fuel the boilers, visitors described Shafter as a surprisingly pleasant place, having good shade and water. The mine at Shafter became one of the most consistently productive sources of silver in the United States. By the time it shut down for good in 1942, it had yielded

Above: *Stone and adobe ruins at Shafter*

Opposite top: *Mine entrance at Shafter*

Opposite bottom: *Shafter cemetery*

Right: *Church at Shafter, one of the few buildings still left in the old town*

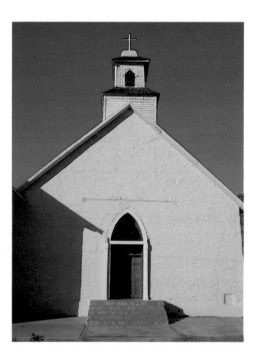

more than thirty million ounces of silver. Though there were other mining operations in the state, Shafter was responsible for nine-tenths of all silver produced in Texas.

There is no silver mining in Texas today. Shafter is a ghost town in the desert. Though its great silver play was a significant strike, its impact on Texas was dwarfed by that of black gold.

The knowledge that oil was present in Texas has been with us since the time of the Spanish explorers who found it floating on the water and used it to caulk their vessels. The first commercially viable discovery of oil was made more than three centuries later in 1894 at Corsicana. Though the field peaked fairly quickly in 1900, producing more than 800,000 barrels that year, it drew the first modern refinery to Texas and established the state as a player in the game.

During the fifteen years after Corsicana, the industry developed sporadically. The upper Gulf Coast around Beaumont had become a popular area for exploration, and in 1901 a driller from Corsicana, Anthony B. Lucas, punched into a wet dome, and everything that had gone before paled in significance. When the Spindletop well blew, it shot 600 feet of pipe weighing more than six tons as high as 300 feet in the air. No one knew how to control such a gusher, and within three days, the well was spewing more than 3,000 barrels per hour toward the sky.

Lucas built a series of increasingly higher levees to contain the immense flow, but even a fifty-acre impoundment would not hold the oil. Nine days after the well came in, Lucas and his men finally got it under control, and the greatest oil boom the world had ever seen had begun. At its peak, Spindletop produced more than seventeen million barrels of oil in a single year.

After Spindletop, exploration on the Gulf Coast and in Southeast Texas proceeded in a frenzy. Oilfield boomtowns sprang up around the play and the scene was unbelievable. Sour Lake was incredibly crowded and the rigs, right up against each other, created a forest of derricks. It was so poorly drained that everything was bogged down in nasty mud created from the slush of hundreds of wells.

During these beginnings, spanning the first twenty years of this century, the oil field began to seriously augment the folklore and myth of Texas. The images of the roughneck, the wildcatter, and the nouveau riche oilman joined the cowboy and the longhorn as the prevailing symbols of Texas.

Taxation of the industry arrived during this period along with the first regulations aimed at conservation. The Upper Gulf Coast remained the center of gravity for the industry, and the major oil companies, most of whom had their origins in Texas, established refining and distribution facilities there. The Houston Ship Channel was completed in 1914, and Bayou City became the global center of the industry.

From there, the play moved north and west, and during the early twenties the largest natural gas field in the world was developed in the Panhandle. At about the same time, a modest well was completed near Colorado City, in 1920, and the next big expansion began to unfold.

During the previous century, the Legislature had, through various actions, established an endowment for the University of Texas by dedicating public lands to that purpose. Nineteenth-century pressure to sell profitable land resulted by 1924 in the concentration of University lands in the Trans-Pecos desert, which then had little value. In 1900 the total income from grazing on millions of acres of University lands in West Texas was only $40,000. All that changed when the well called the Santa Rita No. 1 came in on University property in the Big Lake Field.

On May 28, 1923, the day the Santa Rita No. 1 came in, there were only two oilfield shacks and the rig on the site. Within twelve months, oil fever engulfed the vast Permian Basin. Ultimately there were ten major oil fields. The town of Texon, wholly owned by the Big Lake Oil Company, exploded out of the sagebrush and, by 1930, had a thousand residents, stores, paved streets, a library, a hospital, a public swimming pool, and a golf course. All of that is gone today—gone with the oil and the Big Lake Company that abandoned the site in 1962.

During that long run, numerous towns were completely transformed across the great Permian Basin formation. In the five years following World War II alone, more than 200 new

Oil derrick at site of Santa Rita No. 1, Texon

Abandoned Big Lake Oil Company building, Texon

Street sign in ghost town of Texon

independent and major oil companies moved to Midland, which, although it had no oil fields, was the nerve center, administrative headquarters, and counting house for the basin. Speculation was so intense during the good times that fifty-million dollars' worth of oil deals a year were negotiated in the lobby of the Scharbaner Hotel.

By 1930 it seemed inconceivable that Texas could produce another spectacular discovery, but it happened. On October 6 two colorful promoters, "Dad" Joiner and "Doc" Lloyd, brought in Daisy Bradford No. 3 out of the Woodbine formation in Rusk County and ushered in the greatest oil boom Texas had yet experienced. The massive new flow of oil from East Texas severely weakened the industry elsewhere in the state and compounded the impact of The Great Depression—so much so that both the National Guard and the Texas Rangers were sent

Refinery between Marathon and Fort Stockton

Old Shell Oil headquarters, Midland

in to curtail excess production and distribution of illegal "hot" oil.

Within a few years, production in East Texas stabilized, activity picked up again in the Permian Basin, and the industry generally experienced two decades of steady growth. Technological advances made offshore production in the Gulf of Mexico commercially feasible. During the 1950s and 1960s the cycle headed down again as increasing amounts of Middle East oil entered the marketplace. By some estimates the number of independent producers declined by more than seventy-five percent during this period. Twenty-five percent of the independents in Midland went out of business between 1951 and 1969.

The last big boom came to Texas during the 1970s and 1980s in response to the Arab oil embargo and the creation of the OPEC cartel. Huge amounts of borrowed capital were pumped back into the oil fields in anticipation of ever-higher prices and increased demand. But the huge price increases of the 1970s were also met with reduced economic activity throughout the world, movement to other fuels, increased conservation, and, ultimately, reduced OPEC prices. And though Texas still has one-fourth of the nation's reserves of natural gas, the great oil reservoirs discovered in the twentieth century are largely depleted. These factors precipitated a wave of business failures in petroleum, banking, and real estate in Texas, the impact of which, all too painfully, lingers to this day.

This legacy of surge and subsidence, of miraculous bonanza and unmitigated disaster, is in the cultural DNA of every Texan. It can be best sensed in the empty streets of old boomtowns like Texon and Shafter, which are haunted by how quickly it all went away, and in coffeeshops throughout Texas where talk about the next boom is eternal.

Abandoned courthouse at Sherwood, Irion County

CHAPTER NINE

Government
and
Public Buildings

One of my favorite photographs was taken of the Presidio County Courthouse at Marfa shortly after it was built in 1886. The magnificent French Second Empire structure sits on an otherwise totally empty prairie landscape and is the only object visible against an endless horizon. There is a wonderful expression of confidence in the scene, along with the subtle irony that such a bold public edifice was built in a place with so little enthusiasm for government.

Throughout Texas, the peculiar relationship we have had with government is reflected in our public architecture. Our government structures are statements of civic pride in our communities, of Texans' self esteem, of high ideals and optimism. But the considerable lengths to which we have gone in erecting the structures of state is contrasted with the equal intensity by which we have made sure that the power of their occupants remains limited.

*T*he most essential role of government since the earliest days of Texas has been as referee and recorder of the process by which we own and use the land. Although our concept of land in Texas is philosophical and often even spiritual, it is also very physical. The land is collective wealth upon which everything else has been built, and owning or controlling it has dominated our politics since at least Coronado.

The seat of public involvement in matters of land is the county courthouse, the axis in Texas of our interaction with government.

Here, deeds to land are recorded, along with other vital records of birth, marriage, and death, and surveys and appraisals of the land itself. The district courts administer the justice system, and the sheriff enforces the law. Elections are run out of the courthouse as are decisions to build and maintain the county roads. The commissioners court sets the county's budget and administers the welfare system. This is government up close and personal in a state where, for much of our history, the only federal official most people ever saw was the postmaster, and where even the government in Austin was remote.

County courthouses are ubiquitous in Texas because the state has 254 counties, and many have had more than one courthouse—a consequence of fire, growth, changing architectural fashions, and early "county-seat wars" over their location.

Thus, they are as diverse as Texas herself and reflect the prevailing styles of the periods in which they were built—from Greek Revival in antebellum times to Romanesque and Renaissance Revival in the twentieth. Regardless of style, they reflected the counties' perception of their importance.

A magnificent French Second Empire courthouse stands vacant today in the town of Sherwood, former seat of Irion County. It was the second courthouse in the county. Completed in 1901, the handsome two-story stone structure is crowned by a tower bearing a false clock, set at the presumed time of the death of Abraham Lincoln.

Webb County Courthouse, 1909, Laredo

The hands on the clock could have been set for the death of Sherwood, which withered away when the railroad bypassed the town in 1911. For nearly thirty years, a low-grade county-seat war simmered until Irion County citizens voted to move the seat of their government. The old courthouse stands quietly today in a virtual ghost town, and the affairs of local government are carried on in a modern, if less spectacular, brick edifice in nearby Mertzon.

Along the Rio Grande, Webb County has had four courthouses. The 1909 building in Laredo was designed by noted San Antonio architect Alfred Giles in Renaissance Revival style with Romanesque details. Giles, who also designed courthouses at Fredericksburg and Floresville, was trained in England and immigrated to Texas in 1873. His work, which includes mansions, modest dwellings, ranch houses, public buildings, and

123

Governor's Mansion, Austin

commercial structures all over Texas, drew on a wide spectrum of styles, but his singular vision defines every structure.

Today, eighty-four Texas courthouses are listed in the National Register of Historic Places. All but eighteen of those were built before 1900 and all but twenty-one are still in use. They are a proud legacy of the Texan perception of local self-government in the nineteenth century. Still, nowhere is the contrast between the accoutrements and the reality of power greater than at the Governor's Mansion in Austin.

*P*rior to construction of the Greek Revival mansion in Austin, the first four governors of Texas lived in hotels or boarding houses. In 1854, the Legislature appropriated $17,500 for building and furnishing a suitable residence for the governor. The money was raised from the sale of privately donated lots in Austin. That same year, master builder Abner Cook was retained by a committee composed of Governor Elisha M. Pease, State Comptroller James B. Shaw, and State Treasurer James H. Raymond to construct the Mansion. At the time, Cook was building similarly grand homes with Greek Ionic porticos for Shaw and Raymond. Pease, who was the first official occupant of the Mansion, bought Shaw's house after he left office.

Cook, probably the most significant architect in early Texas, owned a kiln and a sawmill. He made the bricks for the Governor's Mansion in Austin and hauled in pine logs for the columns from Bastrop.

The Governor's Mansion has been improved and renovated through the years with the addition of gaslights in the 1870s, telephones and indoor plumbing in the 1880s, and electricity in the 1890s. In the 1950s, Governor Allan Shivers added central heating and air conditioning, and two decades later, the house was completely refurbished during the first term of Governor William P. Clements. He and Mrs. Clements led efforts to establish the Friends of the Governor's Mansion, which helped finance the restoration, established an endowment, and which now has stewardship of the furnishings and artifacts, under a contracted arrangement with the Texas Historical Commission, which has overall supervision of the site.

The Mansion, like Abner Cook's other structures, displays a monumental elegance and sophistication rarely seen in early Texas since the erection of the missions. It stands today as a monument to the pride Texans take in their initiative and independence. Across the street from the governor's residence, the state executed the climax of nineteenth-century public architecture in Texas, namely, its capitol.

Government has been deliberated and administered in four state capitols in Austin. Plans for a permanent structure were included in the Constitution of 1876, and the competition to select an architect began in 1880. Just two months later, the existing antebellum capitol was consumed in a fire that brought real urgency to the project.

The grand structure—which at the time was one of the largest buildings in the world—was designed in Renaissance Revival style by Elijah E. Moyers, a self-taught architect from Detroit. A contractor was then sought who could construct it in exchange for three million acres of Texas public land in the Panhandle. Mathias Schnell of Rock Island, Illinois, won the contract over just one competitor. Schnell soon assigned the contract to a Chicago firm, Taylor, Babcock, and Company. An up-and-coming builder named Gustav Wilke won the contract for the monumental work.

Myers had specified limestone in his design, but state leaders wanted Texas granite. Stone for the building was obtained from an igneous formation near present-day Marble Falls. In accepting the change order for the new stone, Taylor, Babcock negotiated a new deal with the state in which it would compensate the firm for its increased costs. The state paid for construction of a railroad to bring the granite down from the Llano Uplift and provided inmate labor to quarry the material.

The state agreed to those terms in 1885; labor problems followed almost immediately. The stone cutters' union objected to the use of convicts. In response, the contractors brought in granite cutters from Scotland to cross the picket lines, a violation of the Alien Contract Labor Law.

Texas Capitol and annex

Opposite: *Capitol rotunda*

Above: *Restored House of Representatives chamber, Texas Capitol*

Left: *Texas Capitol staircase*

Despite these complications, the new Capitol was finished and dedicated in May 1888 and formally accepted by the state that December. At that time, the value of the Panhandle lands put up by the state as compensation for the job was less than $2,000,000. The building ended up costing about $3,750,000, so the state contributed $500,000 in addition to the land.

Babcock had visited the real estate to be traded in 1882 when his syndicate was assuming responsibility for the contract from Mathias Schnell. Inspection of the lands took thirty-six days and covered 950 miles. Although the plan was to subdivide the acreage and sell it off as expeditiously as possible, the syndicate chose to utilize the virtually unpopulated grassland and founded the XIT Ranch. At Babcock's urging and with an infusion of British capital, the range was fenced, water wells were drilled, and windmills were erected. By 1885, 781 miles of the XIT had been enclosed, and by the end of the decade, the prairie supported about 150,000 head.

At the turn of the century, cowboys from the XIT were driving more than 12,000 head of cattle a year to pastures in North Dakota and Montana. On the vast ranch itself, there were 300 windmills, 100 dams, and 1,500 miles of fence. But the XIT was never really profitable; the British creditors demanded their money, and the sell-off began. By 1912, the cattle were gone, and the British had been paid. The last of the 3,000,000 acres was sold in 1963, nearly a century after the acreage had been set aside. Today little is left of the XIT, except for the old headquarters building in Channing and the annual XIT Rodeo in Dalhart.

In 1983 the Capitol was almost destroyed when a fire swept through the east wing of the building. The narrow escape spurred a complete restoration of the structure to its 1888 appearance and additional construction of the marvelous underground extension to the north. The total cost of these improvements, which were managed by the State Preservation Board, was approximately $200,000,000.

It was one of the most remarkable projects in Texas restoration history. And the Texas-size swap has ultimately been a winner on the High Plains as well as in Austin. In 1988, at the time

XIT ranch house, Channing, Hartley County

of the Capitol Centennial, the lands set aside by the Constitution of 1876 were valued at nearly $17,000,000,000.

A few blocks from the Capitol, the Texas State Cemetery has also been restored. The state cemetery was established in 1851 at a time when cemetery-museums like Arlington and others were the fashion in America. The first person buried there was Edward Burleson, a hero of the Revolution and Vice-President of the Republic. In the nearly 150 years since, eleven governors and Stephen F. Austin have been laid to rest there, along with Confederate General Albert Sidney Johnston, former member of Congress Barbara Jordan, author J. Frank Dobie, and many others.

Sadly, in that same time, the state cemetery fell into great

131

Crypt of Confederate General Albert Sidney Johnston, Texas State Cemetery, Austin

decline—so much so that at the beginning of the 1990s, it had become an embarrassment to the state. At the urging of Lieutenant Governor Bob Bullock, Texas Parks and Wildlife was assigned to direct restoration and enhancement of the old cemetery, and the project was initiated in 1994. Assembling a diverse group of institutional partners including the General Services Commission, Texas Department of Transportation, the Department of Criminal Justice, and the Texas Historical Commission, the cemetery was rededicated in March 1997.

The San Antonio architectural firm of Lake/Flato conceived the visitor center that was inspired by the old long barracks at the Alamo. The grand but solemn entry gate includes a granite columbarium, and the Memorial Plaza de los Recuerdos honors all those who have contributed to the life and times of Texas. The exhaustive restoration included every headstone in Confederate Fields where veterans of the Civil War and their spouses are interred, most of the headstones on Republic Hill where Austin is buried, and the magnificent sarcophagus of Albert Sidney Johnston sculpted by the noted artist Elizabet Ney.

Barbara Jordan lies on Republic Hill. When she was brought to the state cemetery in 1996, the restoration had not been completed and the grounds were still a construction site. As the cortege moved slowly toward her final resting place, African-American citizens from the East Austin neighborhood lined up at the fence, uncertain if they were allowed to enter, but eager to pay their respects. The gates were thrown open by the construction staff, and the mourners streamed across the hillsides to the place where their heroine would be laid to rest alongside Governors John Connally and Allan Shivers and across from General Albert Sidney Johnston.

It was a moving tableau and a testament to the role of Texas' public places as hallowed but common ground.

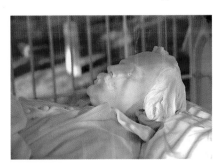

The recumbent Albert Sidney Johnston, sculpted by Elisabet Ney, Texas

Grand entrance to the Hall of State, Texas State Fairgrounds, Dallas

CHAPTER TEN

The New Texas

M y parents brought me to Texas within a few months of the end of World War II. Post-war Texas was alive with opportunity and we were coming home.

They both had grown up in the Depression, and those hard times, along with the war itself, were the reference points for their generation. Remarkably, given all that had taken place, Texas was barely a century old, and perhaps because of that, the themes of its beginnings were also part of the identity of my parents' generation. No concept is more central to Texan self-perception than our sense of independence, and we celebrated the one-hundredth anniversary of the revolution that gave birth to our republic, and our state, during the worst of the Great Depression.

T he idea of celebrating the Texas Centennial began as early as 1900 with a speech by Governor James S. Hogg. Planning began in 1923—when a few veterans of San Jacinto were still around to help locate the places on the old battlefield. Although the limestone obelisk at San Jacinto was erected to commemorate the centennial, the primary focus of the great celebration was on the State Fairground in Dallas.

The first exposition at the place we know as Fair Park was held in 1886. The eighty-acre site in East Dallas became home to one of the most successful state fairs in the country. In 1935, after an intense competition among Fort Worth, San Antonio, Austin, and Houston, an additional hundred acres were added to the site, $25,000,000 were secured for the event, and The Texas Centennial Exposition opened on June 6, 1936.

A Dallas architect, George Dahl, was selected to design and direct the Exposition, and today his work represents one of the most important and largest collections of Art Deco buildings in America. He created a style he called "Texanic," which he believed reflected the strength and boldness of our people's character. Of fifty buildings created for the Exposition under Dahl's supervision, twenty-one were permanent. None so profoundly expresses the intent of its architect or the spirit of the event as the Hall of State. Built by the state of Texas, the monumental chamber at the center of the building is eighty-eight feet from floor to ceiling. In the Hall of Heroes are bronze statues of Austin, Houston, and other giants of Texas independence. On the walls of the Hall of the Six Flags, spectacular murals portray the political, military, economic, and cultural story of Texas.

The centennial celebration brought national attention to the unique heritage of Texas and brought Texas history into everyday life. The stately and decorative architecture stands today as a monument to the perception of Texas as a place of mythic heroes, unlimited opportunity, and infinite resources—a perception which, if anything, was enhanced as Texas was swept, along with the rest of America, into the transformational experience of World War II.

Just prior to the war, as the Centennial was being celebrated, a new generation of techno-entrepreneurs on the Gulf Coast recognized the enormous potential of a vast Texas resource—natural gas. Induced by this seemingly meterless source of power and an almost unlimited supply of water and land, a new and

One of the finest art deco interiors in the nation, Hall of State, Texas State Fairgrounds, Dallas

ultimately climactic industrial area began. An industrial complex soon lit up the skies at night from the Colorado to the Sabine.

For Dow Chemical, the initial raw material was seawater from the Gulf. For many years, Dow had been creating products utilizing chlorine and magnesium from underground brine deposits in Michigan. Fortuitously, about the time the corporation's leadership began to take an interest in Texas, magnesium became strategically critical to the Allied war effort.

In the winter of 1940, Dow purchased a thousand acres of raw Texas prairie at the mouth of the Brazos River. In 1941, following a phenomenal construction effort that is unimaginable today, a Dow employee poured the first ingot of magnesium ever to be taken from the sea.

During the bombing of London, the British discovered that

137

Above right: *Magnesium furnace stacks, Dow Chemical Company, Brazosport*

Above: *Magnesium furnaces, Dow Chemical Company, Brazosport*

Right: *Texas Schoolbook Depository building, now the Dallas County Administration Building, Dallas*

the reason the German aircraft were able to carry such heavy loads of explosives was that they were partially made of magnesium and thus much lighter than conventional planes. Following that discovery, magnesium was elevated from an incidental component of Allied aircraft to an essential one, and Dow's new plants at Texas produced millions of pounds of the light metal for the war effort.

In addition to magnesium, Dow began to make other products from Gulf waters, and the huge supplies of natural gas began to yield feedstock for petrochemicals as well as energy. This was the beginning of a vast manufacturing complex involving hundreds of companies from Louisiana to Brownsville. This system is so extensive that Texas consumes more than twice the amount of energy used each day by the states of New York and New Jersey. The expansion of petrochemicals into every aspect of life brought the coastal regions of Texas unprecedented prosperity, but there were destructive environmental consequences that have not completely gone away.

I grew up on the Gulf Coast in the years immediately following the war. We lived right in the heart of what had been Stephen F. Austin's colony, shaded by the huge oaks of the Brazos Bottomlands. My dad worked for Dow. On the prairies and savannahs where Santa Anna chased Sam Houston, at night you could drive for hours without headlights because the whole region was illuminated by the flares of billions of cubic feet of natural gas being burned off as waste.

I attended a high school set literally among the ruins of Austin's colony. The unlimited promise of Texas and the nation was a state of mind, and as we came of age, a young and attractive new president promised to propel humankind to the moon. John F. Kennedy was not universally admired or accepted in Texas, to say the least, but he chose a legendary Texan, Lyndon Johnson, as his vice-presidential running mate, and assigned him administrative responsibility for the manned space program. The nerve center of this incredible scientific and technological venture was Houston. It was an exciting and optimistic time.

I was in my algebra class when it was announced that President Kennedy had been shot and killed while riding in a motorcade in Dallas. After the President was assassinated on November 22, 1963, the Texas School Book Depository—from where the fatal shots were said to have been fired—was closed to the public for twenty-five years. During much of this period an intense debate raged between those who believed the less said about the assassination the better, and those who believed an obligation existed to preserve the structure and deal squarely with the event with which the city was forever identified. The brick building, which was built by a plow company in 1903, was eventually utilized to house the administrative offices of Dallas County.

In the end, a museum on the sixth floor was opened to the public on February 20, 1989. The nature of the exhibit reflects the ultimate desire of the Dallas community to directly face its history. Today, the Sixth Floor Museum is not just a memorial but an interpretive center that presents the life and death of John F. Kennedy to generations that do not know him. Most of its visitors are people born after 1963. For them it is an opportunity to sort out for themselves the continuing controversies surrounding the assassination and to confront head-on one of the worst days in Texas history.

I left Texas in the sixties and did not return for almost a decade. I remember feeling, when I came back to Houston, that nothing had changed, but everything had changed. I could sit in a restaurant and listen to engineers discuss the technical issues involved with establishing a colony on the moon, while at the same time and at the next table hear that the era of cheap energy was gone for good.

Today the Lyndon B. Johnson Space Center is still home-base for the men and women who fly American spacecraft. Originally known as the Manned Spacecraft Center, the facility has directed the most significant exploration effort in human history and is the location of the Space Station Program Office. In 1992 the Manned Space Flight Education Foundation opened Space Center Houston.

Historic spacecraft are on display along with state-of-the-art interpretive exhibits and tours of the space center. On the grounds, the huge techno-relics lie quietly no more than thirty miles from the spot where Cabeza de Vaca washed up on the beach and began the exploration of Texas—in his day as remote and alien as the moon.

Now the twentieth century is coming to an end, and, along with it, some of the assumptions upon which Texan culture has been based. Though many of those tenets of faith seem as strong as ever, in this century all have been severely tested.

There is no question in my mind that the era of unlimited physical resources in Texas is over. It really has not been all that long since government officials were giving land away to encourage people to come here. Now we struggle to provide enough water for the needs of the present, and our population is expected to double in the next generation.

And yet as vexing as that dilemma seems to be, we've been on this ground before. Ours is a culture rooted deeply in adversity, and we Texans can learn from our history. Since that first ingot of magnesium was poured at Freeport, we've learned to take better care of our resources and the environment as well.

Since that horrible day in November of 1963, we've learned to be more tolerant of each other—an essential trait as the rich ethnicity of those who call themselves Texans continues to diversify.

And though we are a very different people now and continue to change, we are bound together by a need to face the most daunting issues yet and are armed with a great heritage of having done so. At the places where we have met our greatest challenges, our children can touch and understand our greatest values. Among the artifacts of our greatest failures and achievements, they may glean their own sense of independence and self-reliance, and they may gain the inspiration and wisdom to protect their own heritage and continue reaching for the stars.

Saturn rocket at the Lyndon B. Johnson Space Center, Houston

Epilogue

And so on the eve of the millenium, as Texas continues to evolve and we are faced with the difficult challenge of protecting what remains, the sites of our history are the stepping stones along a pathway to who and where we are. And as it has been from the start, we are constantly changing.

In the next generation, our population is expected to double, and the majority of new Texans will have been born somewhere else. They will arrive with little sense of the unique culture of Texas, and even less of our values and history. But they will add new stones to the path and imbue new sites with historic significance.

The places that speak with eloquence of our past take many forms and are as diverse as the history of Texas herself. In caring for them in the future, everyone has a role to play, from members of historical commissions in our smallest communities to business leaders in our largest industries. Preservationists are people who can give money and people who care and vote.

Texas' historical sites need all the energy we can muster on their behalf and all the help they can get. They are in harm's way now. Those which have already been preserved are expensive to operate, and too often they are scenes of unhealthy disputes between those who believe they have exclusive claim to them. Those sites which are not protected frequently lie in the path of other initiatives which, in the name of progress, threaten to obliterate them.

We have no higher obligation than to select the most signifi-

143

cant and representative of these places, protect them well, and tell their story thoughtfully and truthfully. We must remove them from inconsequential controversy and ensure that they convey to future Texans the full spectrum of our experience.

Managing them in the next century will require us to find adaptive uses for historic structures which will make them capable of serving multiple purposes. Such functions should materially contribute to the stewardship and use of these resources, while maintaining their essential integrity and character.

Our policy for cultural resources should move from measures based on control to those based on incentive. We must reward private property owners for protecting their history and make preservation easier for them—not more difficult.

Finally, we must understand that we are making history every day and continuing to weave the tapestry of our culture. The marks we make on the face of Texas will tell our story to future generations. We must be conscious of our impact and remember that one thing that distinguishes us from those whose forebears crossed the Bering Strait and who saw Texas for the first time is that we know those who come later will see what we have done. The artifacts of our culture that we leave to our children will be our most eloquent expression of who we were, what our values were, and our aspirations for them.

It is a wonderful story and a noble responsibility.

Stonewall, Texas
July 31, 1997

Bibliography

Alexander, Drury Blakeley and Todd Webb. *Texas Homes of the Nineteenth Century*. Austin: University of Texas Press, 1966.

Baker, T. Lindsay. *Ghost Towns of Texas*. Norman: University of Oklahoma Press, 1986.

Britton, Karen Gerhardt. *Bale o' Cotton: The Mechanical Art of Cotton Ginning*. College Station: Texas A & M University Press, 1992.

Cartwright, Gary. *Galveston: A History of the Island*. New York: Antheneum, 1991.

Chipman, Donald E. *Spanish Texas, 1519-1821*. Austin: University of Texas Press, 1992.

Clayton, Lawrence and J. U. Salvant. *Historic Ranches of Texas*. Austin: University of Texas Press, 1993.

Cohen, Judith Singer. *Cowtown Moderne : Art Deco Architecture of Fort Worth, Texas*. Fort Worth: TCU Press, 1988.

Colegrove, Bill. *Episodes: Texas Dow, 1940-1976*. Houston: Larksdale, 1983.

Corning, Leavitt, Jr. *Baronial Forts of the Big Bend: Ben Leaton, Milton Faver and Their Private Forts in Presidio County*. San Antonio: Trinity University Press, 1967.

Cypher, John. *Bob Kleberg and the King Ranch: A Worldwide Sea of Grass*. Austin: University of Texas Press, 1995.

Dembling, Sophia. "The Churches of Fayette County." *Texas Journey*. May-June, 1997.

Fehrenbach, T. R. *Lone Star: A History of Texas and the Texans*. New York: American Legacy Press, 1968, 1983.

Fishgall, Gary, Lynn Radeka and Alan Briere. *Historic Towns of America*. New York: Mallard Press, 1992.

Fornell, Earl Wesley. *The Galveston Era: The Texas Crescent on the Eve of Secession*. Austin: University of Texas Press, 1961.

Fowler, Arlen L. *The Black Infantry in the West, 1869-1891*. Norman: University of Oklahoma Press, 1996.

Bibliography

Groneman, Bill. *Alamo Defenders: A Genealogy: The People and Their Words.* Austin: Eakin Press, 1990.

Hardin, Stephen L. *Texian Iliad: A Military History of the Texas Revolution.* Austin: University of Texas Press, 1994.

Henry, Jay C. *Architecture in Texas, 1895-1945.* Austin: University of Texas Press, 1993.

Houghton, Dorothy Knox Howe, Barrie M. Scardino, Sadie Gwin Blackburn and Katherine S. Howe, with introduction by Margaret Swett Henson. *Houston's Forgotten Heritage: Landscape, Houses, Interiors, 1824-1914.* Houston: Rice University Press, 1991.

Hunt, Conover. *JFK for a New Generation.* Dallas: The Sixth Floor Museum and Southern Methodist University Press, 1996.

Jordan, Terry G. *North American Cattle-Ranching Frontiers: Origins, Diffusion, and Differentiation.* Albuquerque: University of New Mexico Press, 1993.

Kelsey, Mavis P., Sr. and Donald H. Dyal. *The Courthouses of Texas: A Guide.* College Station: Texas A & M University Press, 1993.

King, Irene Marschall. *John O. Meusebach: German Colonizer in Texas.* Austin: University of Texas Press, 1967.

Kirkland, Forrest and W. W. Newcomb, Jr. *The Rock Art of Texas Indians.* Austin: University of Texas Press, 1967.

Lack, Paul. *The Texas Revolutionary Experience: A Political and Social History, 1835-1836.* College Station: Texas A & M University Press, 1992.

Laroe, Lisa. "La Salle's Last Voyage." *National Geographic,* May, 1997.

Leckie, William H. *The Buffalo Soldiers: A Narrative of the Negro Cavalry in the West.* Norman: University of Oklahoma Press, 1967.

Lynch, Gerald. *Roughnecks, Drillers, and Tool Pushers: Thirty-three Years in the Oil Fields.* Austin: University of Texas Press, 1987.

McComb, David G. *Galveston: A History.* Austin: University of Texas Press, 1986.

_____. *Texas: A Modern History.* Austin: University of Texas Press, 1989.

McCullar, Michael. *Restoring Texas: Raiford Stripling's Life and Architecture.* College Station: Texas A & M University Press, 1985.

Newcomb, W. W. *The Indians of Texas: From Prehistoric to Modern Times.* Austin: University of Texas Press, 1961, 1973.

Parsons, Mark and R. E. Burnett. *Landmark Inn State Historic Site: Archeological Investigations, Medina County, Texas, 1975-1980.* Austin: Texas Parks and Wildlife Department, 1984.

Prospector, Cowhand, and Sodbuster: Historic Places associated with the Mining, Ranching, and Farming Frontiers in the Trans-Mississippi West. Vol. XI, The National Survey of Historic Sites and Buildings. United States Department of the Interior, National Park Service, Washington, 1967.

Ragsdale, Crystal Sasse. *The Women and Children of the Alamo.* Austin: State House Press, 1994.

Rave, W. J. "Magnesium Production in the Southwest." *Journal of the Electrochemical Society*, vol. 100, no. 7, July, 1953.

Roberts, David. "Sieur de La Salle's fateful landfall." *Smithsonian*, April 1997.

Robertson, Pauline Durrett and R. L. *Panhandle Pilgrimage.* Canyon: State Plains Press, 1976.

Robinson, Willard B. and Todd Webb. *Texas Public Buildings of the 19th Century.* Austin: University of Texas Press, 1974.

Sanchez, Mario L., editor. *A Shared Experience: The History, Architecture and Historic Designations of the Lower Rio Grande Heritage Corridor.* Second Edition. Austin: Los Caminos del Rio Heritage Project and the Texas Historical Commission, 1994.

Sandweiss, Martha A., gen. ed. *Contemporary Texas: A Photographic Portrait.* Austin: Texas Monthly Press, 1986.

_____, gen. ed. *Historic Texas: A Photographic Portrait.* Austin: Texas Monthly Press, 1986.

Schambra, William P. "The Dow Magnesium Process, at Freeport, Texas." *Transactions of the American Institute of Chemical Engineers*, vol. 45, no. 1, February 25, 1945.

Sheffy, L. F. *Francklyn Land and Cattle Company: A Panhandle Enterprise, 1882-1957.* Austin: University of Texas Press, 1963.

Silverthorne, Elizabeth. *Plantation Life in Texas.* College Station: Texas A & M University Press, 1986.

Simons, Helen and Cathryn A. Hoyt. *Hispanic Texas: A Historical Guide.* Austin: University of Texas Press, 1992.

Smith, David Paul. *Frontier Defense in the Civil War: Texas' Rangers and Rebels.* College Station : Texas A&M University Press, c1992.

Smith, F. Todd. *The Caddo Indians: Tribes at the Convergence of Empires, 1542-1854.* College Station: Texas A & M University Press, 1995.

Spratt, John Stricklin. *The Road to Spindletop: Economic Change in Texas, 1875-1901.* Austin: University of Texas Press, 1955, 1988.

Texas Parks and Wildlife Department. *Caddoan Mounds: Temples and Tombs of an Ancient People.*

Torres, Louis. *San Antonio Missions.* Tuscon: Southwest Parks and Monuments Association, 1993.

Tyler, Paula Eyrich and Ron Tyler. *Texas Museums: A Guidebook.* Austin: University of Texas Press, 1983.

Bibliography

Tyler, Ron et al. *The New Handbook of Texas.* 6 vols. Austin: Texas State Historical Association, 1996.

Utley, Robert M. *The Indian Frontier of the American West, 1846-1890.* Albuquerque: University of New Mexico Press, 1884.

"A Visitor's Guide to the Wilson Historic District." Preservation Dallas, Dallas, Texas.

Wallace, Ernest, David M. Vigness and George B. Ward. *Documents of Texas History.* Second Edition. Austin: State House Press, 1994.

Watkins, T. H. *Gold and Silver in the West: The Illustrated History of an American Dream.* Palo Alto, California: American West Publishing Company, 1971.

Whitehead, Don. *The Dow Story: The History of the Dow Chemical Company.* New York: McGraw-Hill Book Company, 1968.

Wiencek, Henry. *The Moody Mansion and Museum.* Galveston: Mary Moody Northen, Inc., 1991.

Williams, Byrd. *Fort Worth's Legendary Landmarks.* Fort Worth: Texas Christian University Press, c1995.

"Wilson Historic District Walking Tour." Preservation Dallas, Dallas, Texas.

A Window to the Past: A Pictorial History of Brazoria County, Texas. Brazoria County Historical Museum and Brazoria County Historical Commission, 1986.

"Yates House." The Heritage Society, Houston, Texas.

"The Zedler Family." *Plum Creek Almanac,* vol. 4, no. 2.

Zintgraff, Jim and Solveig A. Turpin. *Pecos River Rock Art: A Photographic Essay.* San Antonio: Sandy McPherson Publishing Company, 1991.

Site Information

Alibates Flint Quarries National Monument
  Fritch TX 79036
  806-857-3151
Antioch Missionary Baptist Church
  500 Clay
  Houston TX 77251
  281-875-1101
Burton Cotton Gin
  Operation Restoration, Inc.
  P. O. Box 98
  Burton TX 77835
  409-289-3378
Caddoan Mounds State Historical Park
  Route 2, Box 85C
  Alto TX 75925
  409-858-3218
Cibolo Creek Ranch
  P. O. Box 44
  Shafter TX 79850
  915-229-3737
Corpus Christi Museum of Science and History
  1900 North Chaparral St.
  Corpus Christi TX 78401
  512-883-2862
Dallas Historical Society
  P. O. Box 150038
  Dallas TX 75315-0038
  214-421-4500
Fort Griffin State Historical Park
  Route 1
  Albany TX 76430
  915-762-3592
Fort McKavett State Historical Park
  P. O. Box 867
  Fort McKavett TX 76841
  915-396-2358
Fort Richardson State Historical Park
  P. O. Box 4
  Jacksboro TX 76458
  817-567-3506

The Governor's Mansion
  11th and Colorado
  Austin TX 78711
  512-463-5518
Guadalupe Mountains National Park
  Pine Springs TX 88220
  915-828-3385
Hall of State
  Fair Park
  Dallas Historical Society
  P. O. Box 150038
  Dallas TX 75315-0038
  214-421-4500
Historic Brownsville Museum
  641 E. Madison
  Brownsville TX 78520-6071
  210-548-1313
Landmark Inn State Historical Park
  402 Florence Street
  Castroville TX 78009-4018
  210-538-3858
Lindheimer Museum
  491 Comal Street
  New Braunfels TX 78130-7655
  210-608-1512
Manuel Guerra Residence and Store
  Portscheller St. and Main Plaza
  Roma TX
Moody Mansion and Museum
  2618 Broadway
  Galveston TX 77550-4427
  409-762-7668
Painted Churches Tour
  Schulenburg Visitor Information
  P. O. Box 65
  Schulenburg TX 78956
  409-743-4514

Ranching Heritage Center
Museum of Texas Tech University
4th Street & Indiana Ave.
Lubbock TX 79409
806-742-2442

Rice Family Log Home
Mission Tejas State Historical Park
Route 2, Box 108
Grapeland TX 75844
409-687-2394

San Antonio Conservation Society
107 King William St.
San Antonio TX 78204
210-224-6163

San Antonio Missions National Historical Park
2202 Roosevelt Ave.
San Antonio TX 78210
210-534-8833

San Jacinto Battleground State Historical Park
3523 Highway 134
LaPorte TX 77571
281-479-2431

Seminole Canyon State Historical Park
P. O. Box 820
Comstock TX 78837
915-292-4464

Sixth Floor Museum
411 Elm St.
Dallas TX 75202-3317
214-653-6666

Steves Homestead
509 King William St.
San Antonio TX 78204
210-227-9160

Texas & Pacific Terminal
200-300 W. Lancaster
Fort Worth TX

Texas Historical Commission
1511 Colorado
Austin TX 78701
512-463-6100

Texas State Cemetery
901 Navasota
Austin TX
512-463-0605

Texas State Capitol
Austin TX
512-463-0063

Varner-Hogg Plantation State Historical Park
Box 696
West Columbia TX 77486
409-345-4656

Washington-on-the-Brazos State Historical Park
Box 305
Washington TX 77880
409-878-2214

Wilson Historical District
Preservation Dallas
2922 Swiss Ave.
Dallas TX 75204-5928
214-821-3290

Yates House
The Heritage Society of Houston
Sam Houston Park
1100 Bagby
Houston TX 77002
713-223-8367